# ME, POLIO AND
# SCOOT4LIFE

# ME, POLIO AND SCOOT4LIFE

A mobility scooter and a caravan, visiting 150 lifeboat stations around the UK coast in 19 weeks

Reginald Anthony Marchant

First published in Great Britain as a softback original in 2022

Copyright © Reginald Anthony Marchant

Design, typesetting and publishing by UK Book Publishing

www.ukbookpublishing.com

ISBN: 978-1-915338-15-0

# Contents

# Introduction

What you are about to read is a true story which has taken me in excess of seven years to put together using my computer with the aid of Dragon Naturally Speaking. This for me has been a great opportunity to write down some memories of my childhood, plus give you a glimpse of my life so far. But the main story is about Brenda, my wife, Brian, my old school pal, and, of course, myself plus Sam, our pet dog. Sam was rescued from the RSPCA just before Christmas, of 1999. They had estimated his age at the time as somewhere between four and five years. He sadly died aged approximately eighteen and a half years, after living with us for thirteen and a half years, and travelling round the UK with us on this amazing trip.

Brian and I are both polio victims and went to Chailey Heritage School, East Sussex, through the 1950s. During the months of planning the Scoot4life trip, at an Old Scholars Christmas meal, Brian approached me and expressed his interest in the project, mentioning that he would like to join us on this expedition; however at that time we were still looking for a couple with caravan

Sam

experience to join us. We didn't dismiss his request and, as time passed with no other volunteers coming forward, we were happy to accept him as part of the team. I must express my thanks to him for without him Scoot4life would not have happened.

After leaving Chailey Heritage both Brian and I had remained friends, going on camping trips with other friends in our invalid carriages. We would also travel to many places of interest in these three wheeled vehicles; I had an AC and Brian had a Tipping. In 1968 at Brian's wedding to his late wife Edna (also a polio victim), I was their best man. They also raised two daughters and over the years Brenda and I, together with our two sons, would have many outings with them. After the children had grown up, we sometimes spent holidays together, so Brian was no stranger to us.

The plan involved us living in a caravan for what turned out to be 19 weeks. It was towed behind my Motability car after having first checked with our caravan sponsors at the NEC, that my Grand C4 Picasso was capable of the task. Luckily, I had previous experience with towing a caravan, although a much smaller one, and also driving on the road with a mobility scooter. Brian's Kangoo Motability car was used to transport the scooter when I was towing the caravan. It was also used to deliver me and my scooter to a lifeboat station at the start each day's run.

My initial hope was to have something like a minibus, removing the rear seats but leaving three passengers seats, so that we could transport four crew members (including the driver). We would then use a ramp to enable the scooter to take the place of the removed seats, fitting a tow bar for the caravan which would require just one vehicle for the project, but it was not to be.

Throughout the course of this book I have mentioned, here and there, little bits of local history. I have also included some history of the lifeboat stations we visited during our journey and I have tried to be as accurate as possible, but since writing this book and going to print things may have changed.

If you visit Poole in Dorset you will find there the RNLI Training College and Headquarters which supports all the lifeboat stations around the UK and Ireland. The College is open to the public. You can stay the night or just have a meal, explore the building and discover much of what is achieved by this great organisation. Yes, there are paid members of staff to operate this great institution but there are also many volunteers, in particular crew members who sometimes put their lives at risk in order to save others. So for me it was a great pleasure to be able to tour the coast of the UK and raise money to help pay towards the expensive equipment needed to keep everyone safe.

As a polio victim who now suffers from post polio syndrome (something which many people have not heard of or understand), I would also like to support the great work the British Polio Fellowship are doing to help those in far greater need than me. The many hours I have spent on my computer creating this book will have been justified if, through the raising of extra funds via the sale of this book, these messages come across to you, the reader. I hope you find the book both interesting and informative.

# My Story

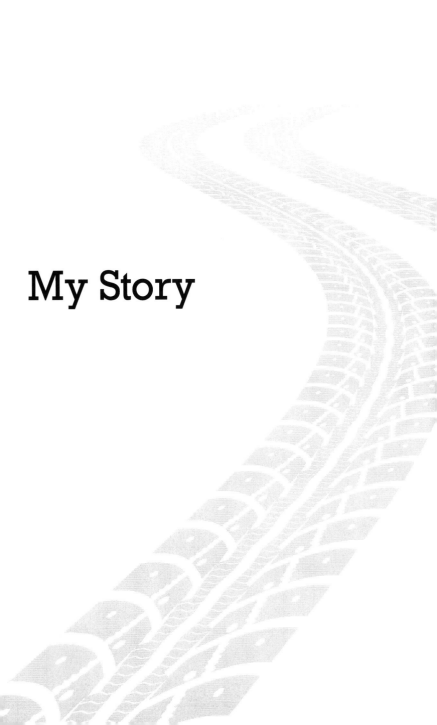

# CHAPTER ONE

# Polio

I started my life having been born in Reading on July 16, 1944 and was named Reginald Anthony Frear Hedges. In 1966 I changed my name from Hedges to Marchant by deed poll just before my marriage to Brenda, but too late for it to appear on our marriage certificate. Marchant was my stepfather's name who, together with my mother, brought me up and so I felt it to be the right thing to do. We moved to Kent very early in my childhood, date unknown, but unfortunately by 1948 my troubles were just about to begin.

At the early age of four years I was struck down by what was called at that time infantile paralysis, now known as polio. It is estimated that 80% of polio victims will suffer from PPS (post polio syndrome). You can find out more about PPS on the British Polio Fellowship website. At this time I was living with my parents in a farm cottage, down a track approximately one mile from the road, at a farm called Somerden, near Chiddingstone Kent.

At the bottom of the small patch of grass next to our cottage flows the River Eden, from where it was suspected that I may have caught the polio virus. However, I believe this was not the case and, to this day, I have no idea where I may have contracted polio.

During one night I wanted to go to the toilet but was unable to get out of bed, so calling out to my parents who came to find out why I couldn't get out of bed. They stood me on the floor only to see me collapse and, realising the seriousness of the situation, an ambulance was called, taking me to Pembury Hospital in Kent (which has now been rebuilt). After isolation and diagnosis I was then sent to a hospital school in Bournemouth called the Victoria home for crippled children, in Almhurst Road, close to Alum Chine. As demand increased for this type of accommodation, new premises were found and purchased and a new home, now called the Victoria School in Lindsay Road, Branksome, Poole, opened in 1958. I stayed until 1952 in Almhurst Road, leaving at the age of eight. My memory of this period in my life is very vague; however, I do know that I spent a long time away from home and only returned twice during the course of a year, at Christmas and for the summer holidays. During my stay at this hospital I have no memory of my parents visiting me, probably because the distance was far too great for them to travel, and they had very slender resources as my father's wages would have been those of a farm labourer.

I remember one occasion I was either travelling home or back to the hospital when the car that I was travelling in was hit by another car. It turned us on our side and, luckily for me, I only had dust in my eyes. Nevertheless a dramatic experience for a child!

I have few memories of my time in Bournemouth but one very significant memory to me was the first time I had an operation. This was performed on my feet. Memory tells me that I was lying on my back, presumably in the operating theatre, when somebody behind me called out my name. As I turned my head to look to see who was calling me, at that moment, somebody squirted water into my eyes. This had the obvious effect of my closing them and giving someone the opportunity to place a mask over my face in order to prepare me for the forthcoming operation. I still remember, to this day the sensation of being in a huge domed building where voices were echoing and remembering the nurse trying to comfort me.

Other things I remember are learning to tell the time and the day a magician came to visit us with his magic wand. I was much impressed and, because of this, desperately wanted that magic wand. I also remember the magic lanterns that were hanging up in the dining hall at Christmas time, eating malt from a great big tin. My stay at this hospital was where I first saw a flying model aeroplane which captured my heart and I wanted one just as badly as the magic wand but, alas, I never got the magic wand nor the model aeroplane. (Later on at Chailey Heritage, I did manage to build my own model aeroplanes made from a balsa wood kit.)

# CHAPTER TWO

# Chailey Heritage

If my memory serves me rightly, when a young male reached the age of eight it was time to move on and so I left Bournemouth and arrived at Chailey Heritage in 1952. One part of my childhood I cannot remember is when I first had to wear callipers on my lower legs which at night were swapped for night splints. On my right arm also I wore a leather splint from my elbow down to my hand but, as time passed, operations reduced these instruments of torture and, in particular, the night splints would disappear. I know these things were necessary and that this was the technology of the day, but as a child they seemed to me torture, as I have described above. I had many operations at Chailey Heritage on legs and feet and also my right arm. I believe some of them may have been experimental.

Chailey Heritage was to be my new second home. My older brother Raymond, who suffered from TB, was already attending Chailey Heritage school. To my knowledge, we were the only brothers ever to have been at Chailey Heritage at the same time in the 1950s. I was lucky to have a brother already there to help me integrate into this new world. It was a place of fierce independence and a place where it was essential to stand on one's own two feet, metaphorically speaking, in order to survive in this new environment.

It was here that I was first introduced to a box of Swan Vestas matches. You could strike these matches on almost anything. How fascinated I was by this! Campfires became an interest to me at a place near Pets Corner at St. George's. St George's, where the windmill stands to this day, is said to be the centre of Sussex. The windmill is now a museum but in the 1950s it was our Scout HQ. Pretty unique I would say. We were allowed to make campfires at weekends and cook potatoes in the ashes. When they were cooked we would retrieve them. They were extremely hot and black on the outside. They would blacken our hands and the freshly peeled parts of the potatoes. I imagine our faces matched our hands.

The practice of having access to camp fires would sometimes lead to setting the common alight at North Chailey. This gave us an excuse to help fight the fire but unfortunately, boys being boys, the fire often seemed to spread across paths to other areas. The consequences were blamed on boys from Chailey Village. I must add at this point that I do regret any involvement in these actions in which I may(!) have played a part. It did however result in us making a fire engine to help put out these fires. This consisted of four old pram wheels, planks of wood and a five gallon drum filled with water with a hose pipe attached to the bottom. It would be rushed onto the common when the next fire needed to be extinguished. Bear in mind our fire engine water system was gravity fed and was to be towed behind a go-kart which we had made previously in the same way, with boy-powered engines! Building go-karts was an obsessive hobby for a group of us, and another one of our projects was building an ambulance. We had made a ladder for the fire engine but not yet the vital stretcher needed for the ambulance. On one occasion, while in the wood, affectionately known as Bandits Wood, situated on the right hand side of the lane approaching St George's and the windmill, my best friend fell out of a tree and broke his leg. Although we did not use our ambulance to take him back to St. George's but when the hospital staff arrived, they placed him on the ladder we had built for the fire engine and carried him back up the lane to St. George's to start his recovery. How proud we were that the ladder from our fire engine helped in his rescue!

If it was your birthday it was best to keep it a secret because it could save you from a cold bath on the day. You can imagine how much of a shock such a bath was to your system first thing in the morning. Luckily for me my birthday comes in July and not in the dead of winter. However, once you had established your position within the structure of the group and were strong enough, you might be able to avoid further birthday shocks.

One of our daily routines during the week was crossing the common from St George's to the Old Heritage, in our shorts and capes, which resulted in me getting chilblains at the top of my legs during the winter months. Arriving at our classroom we were taught not only normal lessons but also woodwork, leatherwork and printing but, during all of these, there were interruptions for physiotherapy etc in the gym. After morning lessons we then would return across the common to St George's, a distance of approximately a quarter of a mile, for lunch and bed rest. We came back for afternoon lessons and then back again to St George's at the end of the day. Interruptions during the school day were common for many of us. For me there was a hot wax bath in the gym into which I had to place my right hand a number of times, slowly building up several layers of wax. This was meant to free-up the stiff knuckles. It was a weekly process and had no effect whatsoever and today my knuckles are still the same as they were before any treatment. However, despite this, the two operations performed on my right arm were successful. One was to turn the hand into a normal position, and the other, a procedure on the ligaments of my four fingers, enabled me to grip light objects in my hand when I moved my wrist back. This operation was the second one of its kind in the country at the time.

Somebody had gifted to the Heritage a car and caravan. The car came to St George's courtyard for the boys and the caravan went to the New Heritage for the children to play in. The car was generally pushed around the courtyard until eventually, bit-by-bit, it was taken apart and, after we had explored it to the full, it was removed for scrap. However the caravan was used as a hideout for some of the boys from Boys Ward who managed to spend two or three days in it undetected by members of staff along with the police who were looking for them. They eventually gave themselves up, probably through boredom and lack of food.

My best subject at school was science or, should I say science was the most interesting subject for me. Whilst on Boys Ward, lying in bed outside at night looking up at the Milky Way (in those days there was very little light pollution), I wondered and had deep thoughts about what I could see. This may have been the inspiration for the interest I have in science and astronomy. I think I may well have bored my science teacher with the hot-air engine designs I came up with, which he explained to me would never work before I would just go away and redesign another one. Well, eventually, I understood the reasons why they wouldn't work and I'm sure he was relieved. In my naivety I designed and built a three stage rocket out of cardboard, hoping to fill it with gunpowder from fireworks which I could scrounge from my pals before November 5th. As you can imagine, of course, it would never have worked and I never got the gunpowder any way, which In hindsight was a good thing!

Another mad invention was building a diving lung. My ambition was to use it in the nearby lake which was down what we called The Dip, across the common and onto farmland some distance away. I did complete it but of course it would not have worked, except in principal, as the inlet and outlet valves were made from the inner tube of a bicycle, which, although they worked, were far too small. Another drawback was that the oxygen compartment was made out of polythene using yet another bicycle valve to introduce the oxygen via a bicycle pump. When inflated and strapped to a person's back it would only act as a buoyancy aid. Well, at least I had tried and I would have probably have saved myself from drowning but I never finalised the means of holding the facemask in place – just as well I think.

At one point during my stay at Chailey, we formed a gang called the Dingle Gang. I believe the name was influenced from watching a film in the Liberty Hut, where films were normally shown on Sunday evenings. The Dingle Gang had their own hut and no outsiders, including the staff, would come near us. The whole thing eventually got out of hand and we were called into the chaplain's office, one by one, and threatened with expulsion if we did not disband the gang. So that was the end of the Dingle gang.

The Dingle gang on top of our famous hut, with yours truly being the one standing upright in this picture.

For me, my time at Chailey was an unhappy time, away from my family for several weeks at a time, during my eight to nine years there. I had many operations, and to my disappointment, I had two consecutive Christmases at Chailey because of operations, although my parents were able to visit for part of the day during Christmas. It has to be said that the authorities gave us the best Christmas they could. We helped to decorate our wards and we had pillowcases filed with presents, as well as those from our parents. But Christmas was never the same as at home. A donkey was kept on the hospital site, at the New Heritage, and on Christmas Day we had a donkey party. The donkey was led on to the ward and was obviously the star attraction. All of us who were left at Chailey over Christmas, for whatever reason, would attend the party.

Me at the Donkey Party, his or her nose at my left ear.

On one occasion before Christmas a group of five of us boys were encouraged to form a skiffle group, myself as the singer, two boys on guitars, one on a drum and one playing bass. You've guessed right, it involved a tea chest and a broom handle with a piece of string! Unfortunately as time has passed I have forgotten the names of the boys in our skiffle group apart from William.

From Boys Ward I would return to St. George's after my recovery from my latest operation, until they decided another operation was needed. I would then be moved back to Boys Ward across the common to the New Heritage once again, here I got to know the boys who were there for long periods of time, sometimes for many years but, like me, many of us would come and go for our operations. I became so used to having operations it no longer scared me and, on one occasion, when the doctor was prepping one of my legs for a forthcoming operation and he explained that I would need to have the other leg operated on at a later time, I asked him whether it would be possible to have both legs operated on at the same time. He said he would speak to the big chief and, to my delight and great relief, when I awoke from the anaesthetic, I found both legs in plaster, which meant that they had been done at the same time as requested. I was once asked to talk to boys who were going to have an operation for the first time and try to calm them and convince them that it wasn't all bad, I'll never be sure that I achieved this but it gives me personal satisfaction that I had tried.

During one of my stays on the Boys Ward, me and one of my good friends Michael Whitman (who sadly is no longer with us since he lost his battle for life at a young age) one morning decided to wait out on the road at the back of the Boys Ward. There we knew our teacher (incidentally a science teacher first and foremost, but not the one I approached with my hot air machines) always walked to work when he could. We were having a crafty cigarette and it seemed a long time with no sign of him so Michael suggested we do a bunk. We climbed the bank on the opposite side of the road and as we reached the top I said to Michael "Here he comes, I can see him now" but Michael said to me "No it's too late let's go", and so we did. We spent the entire day wandering across fields and through woods actually getting nowhere very fast. Whilst crossing a field my name rang out from a nearby farm. As we approached we recognised the person who had called out as being an ex Chailey pupil. We explained what we were doing and he encouraged us all the more to continue with our quest. Of course we did but, as the day drew on, we were both getting very tired and extremely hungry. The only food we had during the day were chestnuts found in the woods but unfortunately, through a misunderstanding with Michael, I managed to eat them all. He was not best pleased.

We eventually arrived at a farmhouse and knocked on the door to ask the way to the road so that we could return to the New Heritage and back to the Boys Ward. The lady who answered the door kindly welcomed us in. After a cup of tea, biscuits and some money for the bus, we left her with our thanks in the direction she had indicated. It wasn't long before one of the farmhands came running up behind us to tell us that a car was being sent from the hospital to pick us up. We waited with him in one of the barns on the farm and we arrived back at the Boys Ward, where everyone was anxious about our whereabouts during the day. We were given a slap-up tea; egg and chips if I remember rightly. As a result of our day out we were summoned before the headmaster to find out why we had run away. I will leave those thoughts to your imagination but we never got told off for our escape from Chailey.

During my time spent on Boys Ward I made lots of friends with those, less fortunate than myself, who were permanent residents there, sometimes spending years on Boys Ward as previously mentioned. So when I arrived for the next operation I was able to join my friends and members of staff who looked after us so very well. This helped to make my stay just that bit more bearable.

Here I have to confess I was sometimes a bit of a bully, after Sunday parents-visiting, especially since mine were rarely able to visit me, I would go around the ward demanding sweets and then, during the week, I would sell them back to boys to make some pocket money for myself. This is something I deeply regret now, but I cannot turn the clock back.

St George's was where the boys of Chailey Heritage lived and slept in dormitories, where we had three meals a day in the dining hall and spent our free time, when not at school or on Boys Ward. I was made a prefect at St. George's, I believe the only reason was to help to calm my rebellious attitude at this time and it had the desired effect.

At the end of the two senior dormitories was a separate small room where the prefects had a radio, It was a place where we could sit and make ourselves a cup of tea. In those days we listened to Radio Luxembourg during the evening. This faded in and out but it was popular, playing rock 'n roll music. We decided that we could take a wire from the back of the radio speaker and run it down the dormitory, connecting up speakers by the beds as we went, so our mates could listen as well. We used the heating pipe which ran down the entire length of the dormitory to make connections to each speaker by scraping away the paint on the pipe and attaching a bare wire to it .A separate wire would link the other connection on the speakers.

There were no radiators connected to these pipes, situated underneath concrete slabs which ran the length of the dormitory. These slabs supported small wooden lockers next to our beds for our personal possessions. Above these at regular intervals were leaded light windows – single glazing of course! Although I can't remember exactly, there were something like twenty or so beds to a dormitory at St George's, with six dormitories in total, three up and three down.

Another thing I made was a loudspeaker. Not very efficient but it actually worked; it was made from just cardboard, copper wire, and a magnet. In those days we could only obtain speakers from old radios and the wire taken from old transformers.

I mentioned earlier the go carts we made from pram wheels, and other bits and pieces. One of the rooms at St. George's, next to the courtyard, was the Hobbies Room. One day I believe it was the Chaplain who asked us to repair his daughter's push bike. However, boys being boys, we had in our possession an old moped engine and decided it might be a good idea to mount this on the back wheel of the bike. Guess what? That's exactly what we did and to our delight, it worked a treat. For those who could ride a bike, each would take their turn around the courtyard before we had to remove the engine from the bike, repair any damage we had caused, and return the bike in good order to the Reverend.

During the late 1950s with rock 'n roll just beginning to establish itself, attitudes slowly began to change. Chailey had been run rather like a military regime with bells and whistles to line us up on the courtyard, in our individual dormitories, before marching us in for our meals. Some of us wanted to wear our own shirts and, in the end, we were allowed to do so at weekends in our free time. We stretched this out eventually to include wearing jeans as well, and not just at the weekends. In the evenings, during our free time, just before I left Chailey, we were allowed to travel on the bus to Haywards Heath without supervision to go shopping, have a walk round, and visit the Cinema. Liberation was finally coming to Chailey!

This is just a very brief account of my days at Chailey Heritage. After leaving I visit at least once a year, just missing the occasional year depending on circumstances, and meet up with some of my old pals from those days through the Old Scholars Association at Chailey. We also meet, other than at Chailey, for our Christmas meal and Summer outings, keeping in touch with each other's lives. (You can visit the Old Scholars website **www.chosa.org.uk** to learn more.)

I would like to mention during my period at Chailey, Ian Dury the famous singer from the Blockheads, stayed for a short period at Chailey as he also had polio; however I have no memory of him during my time there.

At Chailey I developed an interest in many things, such as, space exploration, science and astronomy. However, on leaving, I was unable to read and write, not even my own name. I believe this was partly due to the interruptions to my education because of the various treatments I received, but also due to the fact that I suffer from dyslexia, which was not recognised at that time. I left uneducated, had no O levels and no A levels, but now I have THREE spirit levels (however I don't think they count)! Also my rebellious attitude didn't help. Missing the normal comforts of family love and being away from home for long periods of time, all had an effect.

As well as the good times at Chailey, there were some dark times, particularly in the very early days. But one thing that Chailey taught me, and perhaps one of my greatest achievements, is that of independence despite all my difficulties. Polio has left me with practically no use in my right arm, something like 50% use in my left, and, similarly with both my legs. Also weak throat muscles, approximately 80% lung capacity, a very weak spine and arthritic right hip. This didn't give me any trouble until I was twenty-one and has been gradually getting worse over the years. I had an operation in 1982 and now have the prospect of another operation as the pain begins to return. Despite this I am determined to carry on as normally as possible, with a few aides such as a stair lift, wet room, and of course my scooters.

# CHAPTER THREE

# Marriage and Family

I stayed at Chailey until I was almost seventeen, leaving in the summer of 1960.

Going back now, it was ironically on the day of my mother's funeral, when my eldest brother Raymond and I decided that evening, to go to our local youth club in Edenbridge, to help take our minds off the day's events. It was here that I first met Brenda, and so fortunately for me one love was replaced by another. Cancer had taken my mother away at the age of 42 after battling with her condition for six years. Her loss to the family was felt deeply by my five sisters and two brothers. For me, having missed a great deal of my mother during my childhood, it was particularly difficult to deal with, which makes me especially thankful that I met Brenda at this sad time.

On a happier note, I married Brenda in 1966 after four years of courting on and off. We bought a caravan on Lydens Farm, just outside Edenbridge, where we lived for three years before the farm was sold and the new owners evicted us, on our request. The council found us a site at a place called Pococks Bank near Four Elms, an old isolation hospital turned into flats. There my younger brother Geoff and I had to clear a space for our caravan to stand. This temporary site without electricity or running water lasted several months. It meant our having to collect water from a neighbour and I had to dig a hole in the woods to bury the waste from the chemical toilet. All our new neighbours were very friendly and helpful to us during this difficult time.

In 1969 I sat with my neighbour, incidentally the neighbour from whom we collected our water, to watch the first moon-landing. It was something I could not possibly have missed. We stayed until 3am before going back to the caravan to bed and being half a day late for work the next day.

During this period the council never charged us rent and so Brenda and I were able to save enough money by 1970 to buy a brand-new Daf van. This meant I was able to give up my AC trike and now could travel legally with my wife by my side.

After several months, and our story appearing in a national newspaper, the council offered us a house in a place called Cowden just a few miles from Edenbridge, but within a week or so, they then offered us a two bedroom flat in Manor Road Edenbridge. There we stayed for six years and had our first son. After that we moved into a brand-new three bedroom house where we stayed for a further nine years and where we had our second son.

From there, through the council we managed to exchange into an empty old-style semi-detached three-bedroom council house on the same estate. It is where we are still living today. By now I was running my own minicab service and was in the fortunate position of being able buy my house from the council. Over the next 20 or so years we have been able to improve both house and garden.

During the early years there, a young man of seventeen came to live in our house. He was at school with my sons but unfortunately his life had been turned upside down and he was living on the streets, heavily in debt and in trouble with the police. My eldest son, Tony, came to us one day and asked us if we would allow him to live with us, sleeping in his bedroom. We took him under our wing, found him a job, sorted out his problems and got him on the straight and narrow. He lived with us for ten years, eventually getting married, but unfortunately this wasn't to last. As time passed he met a young lady and they both settled down together producing three great sons. During their first pregnancy they asked us whether we would act as grandparents to their children and, of course, we agreed. We now have three grandsons as well as two grand-daughters from my youngest son's marriage, his wife already having a daughter from her first marriage. Now her daughter has one of her own, making us great grandparents!

# CHAPTER FOUR

# Work

In 1960 my mother had found me a job in a local engineering company in Edenbridge, about two and a half miles from home. I worked there for thirteen years, with a short break with another engineering company, also in Edenbridge, where I spent a few months before returning to my old job.

However, I became so bored that I decided to take myself off to the local job centre and asked to be sent on a rehabilitation course. I ended up in a rehabilitation centre in Croydon where, after an initial assessment, I was found to have a natural ability for electric welding. After the course was over I left my old job and found a temporary position at a company called Cowling Signs where I was put in the packing department. The quality of my work was soon noticed as well as my ability for engineering, which led to me being asked to help out on the engineering side of the business.

Once the company was aware that I was signed up on a welding course for disabled people at Leatherhead, they suggested that if I stayed on at the company they could teach me how to use electric welding equipment. I told my wife Brenda, and because she was pregnant with our first child and didn't want me to be away at this critical time living in at the training college during the week, I was persuaded to abandon the course and took up welding with the company. It wasn't long before I was doing maintenance and other bits of electrical work. Eventually I was approached to work in the office but this is where my spelling really lets me down. I had no confidence working in this area and so refused the offer.

After a while my stepfather, who was working at a company called Eaton Williams, managed to get me an interview for a job in the electrical department. There I spent the next five and a half years, as a semi-skilled wireman. Believe it or not, on two separate occasions I was sent to work on site with a fully-qualified colleague. On one occasion our job was to modify the air conditioning supply units on top of a newly built supermarket roof. Day one was okay because we had access to the roof via the stairs, but on the second day this was no longer possible. We were now faced with a vertical climb up a ladder on the side of the building. My colleague took all the tools up first then came down to assist my ascent. He did this by coming up close behind me as I slowly made my way to the top. I made sure I didn't come down until the end of the day! Day three was the last day and luckily we had access to the roof once again by the stairs. The second job on site was in a building housing large banks of American operated computers used for monitoring the weather. After a day's work in the factory we arrived on Friday evening to start work through the night, modifying the electrical supply unit for the computers. However, although we worked through the night on this task, we ran out of time, and by breaking all the rules, we worked to finish our job with the power switched back on because the operators had said it was essential that they turn the computers on. In my supporting role at this point I was carefully monitoring my colleague's every move – successfully!

Sadly by 1981, the year of the disabled, I was made redundant. Whilst looking for a new job, I did some voluntary driving for the local hospital and, during these few months, people were suggesting that perhaps I should start my own minicab service. I took this on board, investigated the situation, and found that all I needed was to insure my car for public liability. I needed £500 for this which I did not have but my brother-in-law, David, kindly stepped forward with the cash and so, by 1982, I started my one-man minicab service, which I named Eden Valley Cars.

# CHAPTER FIVE

# Eden Valley Cars

After a few months struggling in this new adventure the operation I was waiting to have on my right hip became available. This now caused a dilemma. Should I carry on with my new business or have the operation and have to start all over again? I decided to have the operation; the surgeon decided a hip replacement wasn't necessary at this time but suggested a pin and plate – an old-style solution. After several months of slow recovery, I returned to work and it wasn't long before I was able to support myself as a one-man minicab business.

This lasted almost fifteen years before I suffered with mild depression. It had been creeping up on me, almost without my noticing. With hindsight, I now recognise the symptoms. During those fifteen years, at different times, I had two full-time drivers who were self-employed and, in the early days, several part-time drivers.

Some stories that happened during the time I was running my minicab service are worth recounting here. I had previously been contacted by the BBC to take Jean Rook, the journalist from the Daily Express who lived in Edenbridge, on occasions to the BBC Any Questions radio programs wherever it was being recorded. I also took her as a private customer to airports etc. On one particular occasion, I picked Jane up from her house and delivered her to a private house somewhere in Surrey if my memory serves me correctly. It was for dinner before AnyQuestions and then onto another location nearby from where the programme was being broadcast. We arrived at the house, where they would be entertained with dinner and joining Jean were Sir Geoffrey Howe and Bruce Kent, the one-time Catholic priest turned anti-nuclear-arms activist. I and the other drivers were invited into the kitchen for sandwiches and tea.

I chatted with the other drivers and, as it turned out, police bodyguards During the conversation, I discovered that one of the police officers had been in the hotel at Brighton during the IRA bombing where he was acting as a bodyguard for Margaret Thatcher. You can imagine how interesting I found this experience and, just to add, the other drivers also told me how unusual it was for drivers to be invited into a venue like this. After their dinner, I was instructed to take Jean and Bruce Kent to where the programme was to be recorded. This time we remained with our vehicles until the programme ended and emerged from the back door of the venue. We stood waiting for our individual passengers and were all thanked by Sir Geoffrey Howe before I returned to Edenbridge with Jean Rook.

During my minicab days, I received a call from a man supposedly living in the Tunbridge Wells area, who wanted me to fly to Amsterdam and retrieve some luggage that his daughter had left at the airport, because she'd been taken ill while in the airport terminal. He asked me if he could visit me at my home to finalise the details and to deliver the key of the luggage storage area at the airport. He turned up at the arranged time and explained that, if this job turned out to be successful, there could be other jobs to follow. He left me with 100 guilders to take with me for expenses in Amsterdam airport and it was up to me to arrange a return flight from Gatwick. This I did and on the day of the flight I drove to Gatwick, parked my car and arrived ready for my flight. This took approximately 3/4 of an hour before I arrived at Amsterdam airport and, with the means of releasing the luggage from its holding place, it struck me that I had no idea of its real contents, apart from my customer's description of clothing belonging to his daughter. Now, I'm in Amsterdam, a place where certain drugs are legal, so this got me thinking. I made the decision to ask security at the airport if they would check the baggage by running the suitcase through an xray machine which they did and then gave me the all clear!

With time to spare before my return flight I settled down to lunch and then wandered round the shops and purchased a small trinket to bring back for Brenda. Soon my flight back to Gatwick arrived and, having left the aircraft and reclaimed the baggage, I returned to my car, paid the car park fee and set off for home. I contacted my customer who arrived the next day to collect his daughter's belongings and settle my expenses and fees. I returned the guilders I had not spent (which incidentally was most of it as I had only purchased my lunch with it). He seemed to be happy with my service but I never heard from him again and to this day I question whether I was set up and watched at the airport in Amsterdam with the possibility of using me as a carrier/courier for illegal substances to be brought into the UK!

One more experience which I'd like to share with you was when a call came in for me to collect from an address in the Cowden area, a small village a few miles south of Edenbridge, some clock weights and to deliver them to a professor at a college in Yorkshire. The lady in question loaded them into my car and I set off on a long journey which would take me all day but would be for me a good earner. I arrived eventually at the college and immediately found somebody to ask where I could find the professor. Luckily they volunteered to deliver the weights to him on my behalf and so I returned to Edenbridge.

It was some time later that I had a call from this customer to return to the college in Yorkshire, to collect the clock weights and bring them back to my customer in the Cowden area. This time on my arrival at the college there was nobody around and so off I went to find the professor. When I found him, he was giving a lecture and I had to wait until he had finished before collecting the weights. Eventually they were handed to me in a carrier bag and, as I received them, my arm was instantly dragged down with the force of gravity acting on the lead weights. This affected my back adversly and I could not carry them to the car as I was now in extreme pain. The person who gave me the weights kindly carried them to the car but now I was faced with a long journey home with my back hurting as if I had slipped a disc, something I have experienced in the past. I sat in my car wondering whether I would be capable of driving home but eventually started the car. In my driving position I sit upright and very close to the steering wheel and as my journey progressed fortunately my back pain began to ease. Eventually I arrived home almost without any pain at all; my upright position helped to ease my condition. I returned the weights to my customer who thankfully removed them from my car.

Some time, much later, I picked up a customer from the same area and while chatting to him about this experience found that he knew the lady in question and so told me the story behind the clock weights. Apparently the reason I had taken them to the professor in Yorkshire was to test the lead for radiation as it seems the lead had had a previous life connected to the nuclear industry, in some way!

# How It All
# Started

# Part I – The Idea

Before I tell you about our great journey around the UK, I would like to tell you how it all started. Several years ago my brother-in-law, Raymond, gave me a very old mobility scooter. It didn't last very long but convinced me that it was time to accept the fact that using a mobility scooter was not such a bad thing. So I set out to find myself a second-hand one in much better condition. It wasn't long before my friend Frank had found the answer and he kindly lent me the £500 to purchase the machine. I soon found myself driving around the local roads and realizing how much freedom the scooter could give me. So during this time I began to think about the idea of travelling around the coast of the UK.

The idea came to me early in 2003, after reading a book called "The Sea On Our Left", in which a couple who lived in Tunbridge Wells walked around the coast of the UK – a journey I wished I could do myself.

I began to think about a trip around the UK more and more and this preyed in my mind for many months. At this early stage, on the inside, I began to get excited with the idea, but thought that it would be sensible to wait until I was officially retired before undertaking such a project.

I kept the idea to myself for some time while I thought how I might achieve it. It soon became an obsession in my head and I knew I would have to start talking to people and getting their reaction. Slowly over time, as I spoke to many people, the feedback I got was very positive and, inside me, I could feel the excitement of attempting to organize such a project rising. Now I had to convince my wife, in particular, as well as family and friends. My wife's initial reaction was lukewarm at first but soon she was supporting the idea and putting a lot of energy into helping me achieve the project, Scoot4life.

I thought the best way forward would be to do it for charity. At this point I had not reached retirement age, although I had stopped working due to my disability and other reasons, but thought that we could put the project together in two years.

It was somewhere around 2006, possibly earlier, that I started to discuss the idea with family and friends who might be able to help organize such a project. I gradually talked to individuals about the prospect of travelling around the UK coast on a mobility scooter and it soon became clear that other people were sharing my enthusiasm. I recruited a number of people who I thought would be very helpful in putting this project together and so by 2007 I had my volunteers in place.

In March 2008, at the Old Eden pub in Edenbridge, I gathered a group of old school chums, friends and family, to have lunch and discuss the way forward. The next and subsequent meetings took place at my home in Edenbridge some weeks later when my wife and I would arrange lunch for all those attending. We were soon joined by my eldest son and his fiancée and so the planning of Scoot4life began. The hope was to complete the planning within those two years but actually it took three, as the story will unfold.

# Part II – Planning

Our friends Toni and Marilyn, completely forgot about the preliminary meeting at the Old Eden pub. However, Jim, Ian and Lesley, our treasurer, did turn up. Lesley incidentally informed us that she had breast cancer, as if she didn't have enough to contend with since she also suffered from polio. These meetings were to try to decide the way forward and we agreed to have a meeting at our house every few weeks. This was not always the case later on. Mainly it was Jim and I, with Brenda's help. and we would contact family and friends when we felt it necessary to talk things over with them, to help us move forward and to make certain arrangements. This meant that one or two people in the group needed to travel a fair distance to attend these meetings, so we tried to keep them to a minimum.

Our very first official meeting was held on March 1st, 2008. Toni and Marilyn were the first to arrive, soon followed by Ian, Lesley, and Jim. Tony, my son, Laura, his fiancée. Brenda had been very busy preparing lunch for us all and during this meeting we were able to plan our future meetings and ideas for the way forward with the project.

Jim Burbridge became my right hand man. Jim and I, prior to the first meeting, went to visit the guy who had a mobility shop in Edenbridge at this time and when we told him of our plans, he immediately volunteered to sponsor the scooter, also offering us extras, such as suitable clothing which I could use on the scooter. So at our first lunchtime meeting we were able to tell everyone that we had our first sponsor. What a tremendous feeling I had after meeting our first sponsor! Unfortunately, several weeks later, he had to pull out of the project altogether as he was forced to close his shop, for reasons best known to himself, and so we faced our first disappointment.

We began to form a strategy for moving forward with the project. Our target start date became 8th April, 2010. This was because my youngest son, Terry, had moved his wedding plans from August to April 3rd 2010 so that Brenda and I would be able to attend. My original plan was to leave on the first weekend of April, 2010 but by changing it to the 8th of April meant that everyone would be happy.

We needed to raise funds in order to finance the project. Having chosen our charity, the RNLI, because they had stations all around the UK coast which is where I wanted to travel and especially because of the bravery of the volunteers who took great risks in saving people's lives, gave me the inspiration I needed, if indeed I did need any more encouragement.

My aim was to visit as many lifeboat stations as possible. We contacted the RNLI and met with their South East representative, Lou Purdie. Through her, we obtained permission to use the RNLI charity number and to print sponsor forms which we distributed to the local shops in the Edenbridge area. These clearly stated our intention to raise money to sponsor the trip.

Our first fundraising event was held on 18th July, 2009 to raise money to finance the trip and to celebrate my sixty-fifth birthday. This was held at the old school building in Four Elms Road, Edenbridge, subsequently demolished and replaced by the new Edenbridge centre. Brenda's brother David, being one of the caretakers, managed to arrange use of the Hall, for the price of insurance, which helped reduce the fund-raising overheads. The sum of money raised was close to £2000, which included takings from a raffle. The prizes had been donated by the people who attended the event and I cannot thank them enough for their kindness. The entertainment was a disco, with food laid on by Brenda and myself. Up until now we still had no major sponsors, other than our website sponsors, but I remained optimistic during these early days.

Our second fundraising event was a cream tea in our garden, on August 29th, 2010. Though the weather was not kind to us on the day, we had previously managed to erect two gazebos, and with the use of our small summerhouse managed to carry on successfully. With the help of a raffle and the sale of some of my pictures from my past photography expeditions, we managed to raise a reasonable sum of money towards the cost of the trip.

Our third fundraising event was on October 2nd, 2010 again in the old Edenbridge School in Four Elms Road, where once again my brother-in-law David, came to our rescue with the same arrangement as before. We arrived with family and friends at two in the afternoon to arrange the hall for the evening, with a disco and a local band. Eighty-one people came and enjoyed the evening's entertainment, raising more money for the project, a further £982. Even the band (North of Eden) returned the money they were going to charge for the evening, and so this proved to be another success.

Our last major fundraising event was on February 12th, 2011, a Saturday afternoon. We hired Ricards Hall, just off Edenbridge High Street. We invited other small organisations to come along to a tabletop sale and sell their products, charging them a small fee for their pitch, This was once again a reasonable success although we did have to drag a few people off the street and into the event. We sold coffee and tea, cakes and biscuits. By the end of the afternoon we came away with £350 including all the money the small business had collected and given to us towards the project.

I must mention all the local residents, friends and family, who made personal donations before and after the trip, and express my sincere thanks to them for helping to make this unique experience possible.

# Part III – Mobility Scooters

One of the things we needed badly was of course a powerful mobility scooter. On June 21$^{st}$, 2008 we had our third meeting, with eight people in attendance, to decide who would do what and when. In the meantime, I had spent a lot of time on the Internet, plus printing sponsorship forms, and writing letters to major companies around the UK, but without any success.

One day while Jim and I were searching the Internet, we came across a company in Blackpool and decided to ring them to ask some questions about a particular scooter on their website. The conversation ended up with us telling the guy what we were trying to do, and he decided that he wanted to play his part in the project by sponsoring the scooter. So we thought we had our scooter but, as time passed, he became very unhappy about the slow progress we were making. He suggested we used Facebook and Twitter etc, but unfortunately we were not familiar with such things, hence our slow reaction to them. In the end we had an email saying that he was pulling out, leaving us back at square one. Although we had been disappointed again by a scooter sponsor pulling out we were far from giving up. Jim would visit my house on odd occasions to help me with writing letters searching the Internet, etc.

On March 7th, 2009 Scoot4life meeting number seven took place. We were joined by Lou from the RNLI. We had a long chat with her and she promised to help where she could, she suggested that she could arrange a photo shoot in front of the lifeboat at Hastings.

I had posted lots of letters to companies asking for sponsorship regarding the scooter but they had each been met with a negative response. The Scoot4life meeting on 24th April 2009 was our 8th meeting and with just under a year to D-Day we still no major sponsors to announce at the meeting.

On 22nd August, 2009 we arrived early at Hastings We hired two mobility scooters, one for me and the other for my brother-in-law Ray. Ray, with his excellent photographic skills, took the photos for using in our advertising leaflets. At the same time we had arranged to meet Meridian Television, the South East TV company, who interviewed me at the station.

Me at Hastings lifeboat station was the main photo used during our campaign.

We also met Graham and a colleague from Greenmeanie, the company that built and ran our website, during

Me and Meridian Television, the South East TV company.

the three years it took to put the project together. I had previously researched and contacted them after checking on the Hastings lifeboat website and found that they were their sponsors. They kindly agreed to sponsor me as well. After an initial fee of £60 to register the site, they ran it for free and by January 2009 the website was almost complete.

# Part IV – Delays

Frustratingly things were actually going pretty slowly. So on Sunday 22nd November, 2009 trying a new idea, both Jim and I delivered leaflets to factories around Edenbridge in the hope someone might sponsor the project, but there was not much success there either. By July 9 my son Tony had put my interview with Meridian Television on YouTube, trying to get the project out there in the hope this would bring in more sponsors.

With our target date looming and still no major sponsors, we now realized that the trip would not take place in 2010 as planned. We decided to carry on with the project for one more year, in the hope of finding our much-needed sponsors. Fortunately this delay enabled Brenda and I to attend our son's wedding without the pressure of having to travel around the UK a few days later.

June 5th, 2010 at the Edenbridge Festival we had a pitch for a tent where we displayed some of my photographs. We put them into frames in the hope that we could sell them and raise more money for the project. We spent the whole day there and collected a few pounds in donations as people learnt about our project but unfortunately no pictures were sold; however we were featured in the local newspaper, the Edenbridge Courier, as they had covered the event.

While searching on the Internet we found a scooter which we thought might be appropriate for the project and decided to visit the company in Margate, Kent without letting them in on our plans. On arrival I tested the scooter and felt that it would be fine for the job at hand. Later we contacted them and asked them if they could help us with our project. We weren't blanked immediately because of this suggestion and they did give it some thought, but eventually decided that they could not help us, as they were a small business with a limited turnover. We were however grateful to them in the end, because they gave us the lead which we badly needed to find a scooter sponsor. They gave us several telephone numbers of important companies in the UK which we could approach.

On the 26th of May 2010, while scrolling through my emails for Scoot4life, I came across a company called Chichester Caravans, one of the many companies I had written to. The Director, Mr John Bolton, asked whether we had a sponsor for the caravan yet and left a contact number for us to reply. I immediately phoned John and told him that we were still looking and he immediately promised me that he would supply the caravan for the entire journey around the UK, and would confirm this by letter, which he did. We later arranged with him to go to his headquarters in Bromsgrove near Birmingham and on the 23rd August, 2010, Jim and I arrived at Bromsgrove, where we met John to discuss the project and the loan of the caravan. At last things were looking up!

Using a telephone number passed on to us by the mobility company in Margate, Jim and I contacted a mobility company called Days Healthcare in South Wales. We mentioned to them that we had a website, plus a sponsor for the caravan, and this may have persuaded them to want to help. We arranged to visit them on January 11th, 2011. After another long journey to their offices and warehouse, we were warmly welcomed and shown the ST5 Strider mobility scooter. I was invited to try it out and found it to be comfortable. However the controls were right-handed and when I mentioned this to the manager and his female assistant they said this could be changed by computer to left-handed use. They were very obliging also saying that they would supply a cape and urine bottle, in case of emergencies. The scooter was a demonstration model and they arranged to have it delivered to Kent Mobility, just a few miles from where I live.

# Part V – NEC Exhibitions

Part of the deal with Chichester Caravans, was for me to go to the NEC and join John and his colleagues on their stand at the Caravan Exhibition. This meant finding accommodation for six nights during the first of two Caravan Exhibitions I attended. I found a small hotel with outbuildings where I was able to hire a room, very close to the Exhibition Centre. John's colleagues, designed a big poster advertising their support for our project for all to see. I spent the days handing out leaflets I had printed trying to attract a couple to join me and Brenda on this estimated six months project but nobody came forward. I suppose six months is a long time to commit to living with strangers, but it was worth a try.

On February 21st, 2010 I left Edenbridge on my second adventure to the NEC. Following a conversation with John's colleagues trying to arrange a caravan for my stay over at the NEC and for some reason not being able to achieve this, in the end John offered me accommodation at his home, which turned out to be his daughter's flat, a converted building in his garden. While she was at university she had other sleeping arrangements but would join us at the NEC now and again to help John out. At the end of the day we would leave the NEC and return to John's Bromsgrove HQ, dropping off his salesman, before heading out to John's local pub for dinner, a group which included John, his partner Kath, one or two salesman, and sometimes members of John's family, afterwards returning to John's house.

On one occasion, at John's local pub, we ordered our meals and were waiting for them to arrive, the usual chat was taking place, I was sitting opposite Kath and on my left one of the reps was talking to her about operations they both had had recently. Unfortunately, I began to feel hot and bothered and, just as my meal arrived, I had to leave the table because I was about to faint. This was extremely embarrassing for me and I was led out to the entrance of the pub, where there were a few chairs on which I could lie down to recover. Afterwards I was full of apologies to John and the rest of the party but John was only interested in my well-being and was very concerned for me. So I had missed dinner but on our arrival back at John's house and feeling a lot better, I was offered a sandwich, so I had something to eat that evening in the end. This was not the first time this kind of thing has happened to me, being one of those people who cannot watch operations or even injections on the television, particularly when they involves blood. I cannot be sure whether this has anything to do with my experiences as a child.

Back on a more cheerful note, on one of the days during this week, I was volunteered to pick up the reps from John's HQ at Bromsgrove, and drive them to the NEC. John was staying behind to collect his grandson and his grandson's friend, to bring them along later as he had promised the boys. After being introduced to me, they became very enthusiastic about my project and helped me give out my leaflets and collect money from passers-by using the collecting tins the RNLI had supplied to me.

The two boys pictured here with me.

One morning when we arrived at the NEC John took me off to show me several caravan layouts. He told me I could choose any internal layout I liked but I stuck to my original idea; in hindsight I made the wrong decision, however things worked out well enough.

One thing John mentioned to me, and I'm not sure whether he was joking or not, was that he would like me to be at all of his caravanning exhibitions, and I take that as a compliment! Whilst at the NEC other traders were interested in why I was on John's stand, handing out leaflets. One day I was approached by Jim, sales and business development director of Westfalia UK Ltd. This company sells towbars, and other products I am not aware of, and, after chatting with me, and learning about Scoot4life, he offered to send to my home, a towbar free of charge. I am grateful to Jim for that.

My youngest son, who worked at a local company called Whitmore's, dealing mainly with Vauxhall cars, managed to persuade his manager to have the towbar fitted there. He agreed to do this for free, providing we advertised their company name on the caravan and after contacting John for his permission, they did so. They also managed to persuade a company called Indespension based near Redhill, to connect up the wiring for free. There are good people out there ready and willing to help a good cause and I thank them all.

# Part VI – Getting Closer

Returning to January 15th, Jim was at my house on the computer with more emails to do. The run-up to the project start date was getting ever closer. On January 22nd, 2011 Brenda and I left home to go to Godstone camping shop to buy me a waterproof coat, which of course would be essential for the trip. On January 29th Jim came round helping to tie up a few loose ends and by February 8th, 2011 our Scoot4life bank account was in place and ready to go. On March 1st, 2011 Brenda and I went shopping for the last bits and pieces needed for the caravan.

March 3rd 2011 turned out to be an interesting day since it was the day the scooter from Days Healthcare was delivered to Kent Mobility. It would be ready for me to collect, once they had managed to change the electronics and make the hand controls left-handed, unfortunately, this had not been done by Days Healthcare.

On my way home I called into a garage for fuel, putting petrol into a diesel operated vehicle is not a good idea and I realised my error after a couple of gallons but decided to fill the tank with diesel, hoping for the best. I found the car drove perfectly well with the fuel mix, but mentioning this to my youngest son Terry, he advised me to call the RAC to drain and flush the tank through, which they did. It was the fifth one they had dealt with that day; apparently it is most common with the police because they swap their vehicles regularly. I however was getting used to using a diesel operated vehicle for the first time.

On March 6th 2011 we arranged to collect Jim and drive down to Poole in Dorset, a journey of two and a quarter hours. There we met Lou at the RNLI HQ, had lunch with her, and discussed the forthcoming event. after this we drove to a caravan site next to Corfe Castle where we had arranged to spend our first two nights, and also negotiated a small discount. Before returning home, we drove to Swanage, to find the lifeboat station – number one on my list.

On Frank's suggestion, we bought a portable freesat TV system to use in the caravan and he came round on March 8th at 10 o'clock to help put the system together and enable us to familiarise ourselves with it. After lunch Frank returned, this time to work on the scooter. Brian had been down to check how the scooter would fit in the back of his Kangoo, which had a dropped floor and ramp specifically designed for wheelchair access but would also be capable of loading a scooter of a certain size. The scooter I was going to use on the trip was one of the larger types and we needed to know whether this would fit in Brian's car. At our first attempt to load the scooter, it appeared too big, however, by moving the two front seats forward slightly and then stopping the scooter from rolling back by means of wedging the rear wheels, it was possible to lift the ramp and close the door. This was a huge relief at such a crucial time, knowing that this part of the planning was successful.

On March 11th, 2011 Frank returned for two hours, to continue working on preparing the scooter for the trip. That afternoon Brenda and I drove to Maidstone to the DVLA office, to obtain a tax disc for the scooter, and fortunately, there were no hiccups in doing this. On March 12th, 2011 once again Frank came round to continue preparing the scooter, working on the ironwork at the rear. Brian arrived at 12:15 with his girlfriend, our greatest critic; they came in for a cup of tea before we all went to the fish and chip shop for lunch. Brian left with his girlfriend to show her round the local area, to see some of our local points of interest, such as Hever Castle, with its magnificent gardens.

March 15th D-Day was advancing quickly. Frank came round once again to continue with scooter preparations. We had designed a metal T-bar to which we could attach a converted fishing rod to act as a flagpole, as well as orange flashing warning lights. These never actually worked during the trip, except when being transported in Brian's car when we removed the T-bar from the scooter and it lay on its side on the floor. During the trip I took the orange warning lights apart several times but could never figure out why it would not work in the upright position. Jim came round the following evening to spend an hour on the computer, sending emails.

On March 19, 2011 Brenda and I drove to Halland to meet up for a meal with my friends from my school days at Chailey Heritage. It was to wish us good luck for our journey around the UK. Brian and

Liz arrived late. Brian, who lived in West London, had had to drive across to Hackney to pick up Liz, and then head south, to join us at Halland.

March 30th, 2011 was a big day. The caravan arrived at three pm delivered by John personally. After a cup of tea and presenting Brenda with a box of chocolates, he proceeded to show us all the ins and outs of the caravan. It all seemed to happen very quickly and, as a consequence, not all the details were remembered. After John left and before our evening rendezvous at the Old Eden, we began the process of moving the equipment needed for the trip, Later Jim joined us at the pub to wish us well on our journey now with just one day left before leaving Edenbridge.

March 31, 2011. Brenda and I spent all morning loading the caravan with the rest of the various bits and pieces needed for our trip. Lynda, our friend, whom we have known for twelve years, arrived to practise towing the caravan. She would be joining us for a week during the trip to help with the towing. We hooked the caravan up and off she went round the block with me by her side, to get a feel and the experience of towing and so I could have a rest from this task. She picked up the basics very quickly. We returned home and parked the caravan so we could continue loading. Lynda said her goodbyes and returned to her home in Tunbridge Wells.

Frank arrived in the afternoon, as I had arranged to pick up some extra batteries for the scooter to help increase its mileage. Off we went to Uckfield, where Chichester Caravans had one of their seven showrooms, to collect two batteries and then return home to fit them onto the scooter. Frank had pre-wired the existing batteries so that they could be linked to the new batteries. Incidentally these were just ordinary heavy-duty leisure batteries, the type used in caravans, It was well into the evening, before we finally secured them and linked all four together, with the means to unplug and charge them in their pairs. Two battery chargers would give us the ability to charge all four batteries overnight at the same time, speeding up the process.

Friday 1 April, 2011. Friday morning arrived and so did Terry to help us with the finishing touches loading up the caravan. He was soon joined by Frank, Ian Bridle, Ziggy from the local newspaper, Laura from the Edenbridge Chronicle, Brenda's mother and father, and her brother David, and Brian. By 2:15 pm that afternoon we had said our goodbyes and were on our way to the caravan site opposite Corfe Castle. There we had booked two nights stay at a reduced cost as mentioned previously, our first bonus of the trip. We arrived at Corfe Castle at 6:15 pm. We had a little help from the people who ran the site to position the caravan and Terry stayed with us the first night and helped check it out. As previously mentioned, John had given us a quick rundown on how to operate the caravan, hot water, shower, cooker etc, and we had tried to remember everything but were like a bunch of amateurs. After all the fuss had died down, we were very hungry and so we drove to Poole, had a hot meal, bought an electric kettle to use in the caravan, then returned to the site and, as my wife put it, slept 'iffy'!

# AT LAST
# WE'RE OFF!

# CHAPTER SIX

# We`re OFF!

## Day 1, April 2

Saturday morning arrived, Terry got up early and managed to get the water pump working so it wasn't long before we had our first cup of tea. We were still having some trouble with the hot water and sorting out the gas. Fortunately, a man from another caravan eventually helped solve these problems, which helped both Terry and I feel more at ease and so we could move on with the morning plans. We drove into Poole by 10 am to meet Brian, who had been staying with his sister there and looking after the scooter in his Kangoo. Lou from the RNLI and Meridian Television were also at the RNLI Training College to film an interview with us. After we had breakfast at the College, Tony and Laura arrived with their dogs. We all drove back to the caravan and, after a quick turnaround, Terry drove Brenda and me back to the RNLI College, from where we planned to launch Scoot4life. We were met by our neighbours

Barbara and Michael, and friends and family, there was a photo session and then we said our goodbyes.

Now there was only the four of us; Brenda, Brian, me and Sam, our pet dog, I left on the scooter around 2 pm and about three miles out I was surprised to find Tony and Laura stopped in a lay-by and filming me. I had a chat with them and they wished me luck once again, before I carried on with my exciting journey to Swanage. It was a two and a half hour journey from Poole and I was very cold on the scooter but, despite this, I felt good that finally the project was up and running. Down the A351 I passed through Wareham and continued south through the roundabout where the A325 spurs to the right. I was still feeling excited at what lay ahead on this project. On my right, I passed Corfe Castle which stands majestically overlooking the picturesque village with its beautiful cottages on either side of the road. I had no time to visit this National Trust treasure full of its ancient history but in my head I had plans to visit it in the future. Shortly after leaving Corfe village I crossed the road bridge which spans the Swanage Steam Railway. I stopped there for a while hoping to photograph the train but unaware of the timetable and so I eventually left without a picture; however I still felt upbeat about the project and the photographic opportunities to come.

At Swanage where the sea was in a gentle state, I turned right along the promenade to meet Brenda and Brian who were waiting for me at the lifeboat station. Whilst waiting for me to arrive, Brenda had taken photos of the lifeboat station and the surrounding area, When I arrived, I was still feeling excited and apprehensive at the same time at the beginning of this massive adventure. Swanage lifeboat station is an unmanned station and so nobody was there to greet us but we were prepared for this and, indeed, found that this would happen time and time again. After driving the scooter up into the back of Brian's Kangoo, we returned to the caravan where we settled down for the evening and talked over the plans for the next day.

## Day 2, April 3

I was up by 8 o'clock to let Sam out of the door on a retractable lead so that I could reel him in without having to leave the caravan. This operation was carried out extremely carefully as sometimes I was not dressed appropriately. I would then make the tea and get everyone up, washed and dressed, so that we could have breakfast and prepare ourselves for the journey ahead. Being the 3rd of April, it was my youngest son's and his lovely wife, Nae's, first wedding anniversary (I mentioned earlier that they had brought their wedding forward from 2011 to 2010). It was also Mothering Sunday, and so Brenda was opening cards and text messages from both our boys. We finally got the car and caravan together but found it quite hard work, since we were not yet used to the system. With me towing the caravan and Brian with the scooter loaded in his Kangoo, we were finally ready to leave for Weymouth.

After a relatively short journey, we arrived at our next site at Haven Holidays near Preston just before noon. The plan was to move the caravan on a day-to-day basis but as I soon came to realise I was the only one who could tow the caravan, this was to prove impracticable. My second role in this project was to use the scooter to visit as many lifeboat stations as practically possible in a day. We settled the caravan on site without too much trouble. We would let the jacks down using a battery-powered drill which proved to be very successful in making light work of this part of staying and leaving from site to site.

We had our lunch and then Brian and I went for fuel. This came out of our budget set aside for this purpose which also included the site fees. After this Brian and I left to go to my chosen starting point at the junction of the A352 and the A351 near Wareham. I saw no point in returning to Swanage as this would have resulted in us using more fuel. and I had originally hoped to do the project with just one vehicle, so already our fuel costs were more demanding. We stopped in a lay-by next to a bridge over a stream. I climbed into the back of Brian's Kangoo with the ramp down and drove out backwards. Then we fitted the iron work and assembled the flag, umbrella holder, etc, before I set off on my journey to Weymouth, taking a detour on the B3070 sticking to the coast as much as possible. Once again I was feeling quite cold but cheerful. There was no rain which is always a bonus when sitting on the scooter without a protective covering over the scooter itself. The reasoning behind this was to limit the effect of the wind on the scooter and my ability to control it, using only my left hand.

I passed through the village of East Lulworth on the B3070 with its 17th-century mock castle, now a museum, nestling in Lulworth Park. Sticking to my route I turned left at Lulworth Camp heading now towards West Lulworth. Here I turned right, resisting the temptation to visit the famous cove, which if my memory serves me rightly is down a steep hill which would have proven a challenge for the scooter on the way back up. I continued along a narrow back road which, after about half a mile turned inland towards the A352. There I turned left to my destination for the day. It was still cold on the scooter but it didn't seem to matter what I was wearing and didn't deter me from the days ahead. I finally arrived some two and half hours later, having soaked up the atmosphere on the way to Weymouth's unmanned lifeboat station. There Brenda and Brian had managed to collected a small donation. It wasn't long before we found a warm cafe and had a hot coffee, returning later to the caravan. We decided to have a take away pizza from the site and, after finishing our meal, we tried the dongle on the laptop for the first time. Tony tried to Skype but with little success; despite this we managed to get our emails sent. We then talked through the day's events, before showers and bed.

## Day 3, April 4

As usual, I was up first and made tea for the crew which was to become a very familiar pattern. We finished our breakfast by 10 o'clock and then it was time to leave but we were struggling to hitch the caravan to my car. Finally, after a little assistance and chatting for ten minutes with our helpers, we were off! We travelled to our next site at Monkton Wyld, near Charmouth, a lovely site, but once again we struggled and needed help to park the caravan. Obviously a lot more practice was necessary! It was a sunny day but a cold one and Brian and I took care of the usual utilities, while Brenda made our lunch and a nice cup of tea.

By 1.45 Brian and I left to go to the drop-off point at the junction of the A35 and the A3052 to Lyme Regis. Brian returned to collect

Brenda and drive to Lyme Regis Tesco Express for supplies before returning to the caravan and unloading the shopping. They then came to meet me at the Lyme Regis lifeboat station. Those of you who know this route will know how steep the hills are. As I climbed the hill on the A3052, the scooter got slower and slower until it finally reached the summit and I just managed to keep it going before the motor automatically cut out due to overheating. I was immensely relieved, but was beginning to understand the scooter's hill-climbing capabilities and knew that there would be many hills to face on the rest of my journey. However, the next section of this day's scooting was all downhill and what a hill it was!

I was now relying on the scooter's motor for braking! Since the handbrake was fitted on the left hand side of the steering column and, as mentioned previously, I could only operate the controls with my left hand, I therefore had no way of using the manual brake; however my descent towards Lyme Regis was calm and without incident. The automatic braking system worked like a dream and as I neared the end of the descent, my confidence in the scooter's ability grew ever stronger. I finally arrived on the promenade where there were a number of people all dressed suitably against the cold wind. I made my way along the promenade to the lifeboat station, which had a shop on site, where I met a lady volunteer and told her about our project while waiting for Brenda and Brian to arrive.

After managing to park the car in a car park behind the lifeboat station Brenda and Brian joined me at the front of the unmanned lifeboat station, where we waited around in the hope of collecting a few pounds in donations, but had no luck. With the weather being against us and feeling chilly, it was an easy decision to return to the car, load the scooter on board and go back to the caravan for our evening meal.

Tony phoned to tell us that a customer on his window cleaning round had donated £30 to the RNLI and so all was not lost that day. That evening and through the night it rained and the wind blew in gusts, so we didn't sleep very well with the elements battering the caravan.

# CHAPTER SEVEN

# The South West

## Day 4, April 5

With breakfast over, it was still raining and windy but it was time to move on. Brian wound up the four caravan jacks then put all the empty utility barrels and equipment into the back of my car and we hitched up the caravan; this time more successfully. Having broken camp we set off for Haven Holidays caravan site at Devon Cliffs near Exmouth.

Unfortunately we missed the turning and having to find somewhere to turn round is not very clever when you're towing a long caravan, so we lost some time but eventually arrived on site. When reversing the caravan onto the pitch I could smell something bad coming from the car; this was to plague us further on to a point where I thought the project would come to an early end. More will be explained later. With the caravan in position Brian and I set about the task of lowering the four jacks to level the caravan. This allowed

Brenda in to start making lunch, leaving us to sort out the water supply and connect the waste water container and the electrics before finally we had our lunch. Then Brian and I left rather late by now and it was mid afternoon before we arrived at my starting point for the day with the weather rather cold and windy.

I began my journey to Exmouth lifeboat station along the B3178, a relatively short journey through country lanes and hedgerows with their bright green new foliage just beginning to appear, giving me that great feeling that spring had arrived and summer was on its way. I was checking carefully ahead to make sure I did not hit any potholes because a flat tyre would surely be a disaster, especially at this early stage in the project, or at any time for that matter. It would be most inconvenient especially knowing we had no backup for the scooter, and could mean losing a day or two to find a replacement. After another cold journey for me, I arrived before Brenda and Brian but there was no one on site. Not long after, Brenda and Brian joined me at the lifeboat station and with the scooter now safely in the back of Brian's car, we returned to the caravan, where Brian cooked sausages, beans and mash for our dinner. Brenda did a little shopping on site and after dinner we tried the Internet again but with no luck, although we did have lots of text messages to go through and think about.

## Day 5, April 6

We woke to a beautiful warm sunny day with a big blue sky. After breakfast when we had cleared away, I decided to drive the scooter from the site to Teignmouth lifeboat station. This was going to be a long trip, approximately three and a half hours, but it was a pleasant one which I thoroughly enjoyed and for me that was what the trip was all about. The freedom I experienced on the scooter was the same as a walker would have had, exploring the wonderful countryside which lay before me, plus there was the added bonus of raising money for the RNLI.

On this part of the journey I had to avoid the M5 motorway and find a bridge across the river Exe. After leaving the site I first travelled along the A 376 travelling through several small hamlets until I almost reached Clyde St George. There I turned left onto a narrow back road and, after several hundred yards, turned left again, bringing me close to the river Exe. I followed the road into Topsham, an interesting riverside village. Finding the right road through Topsham was slightly difficult but I managed to get directions from a local man. I eventually came to a wider stretch of road but hesitated for a short time because on the road I needed to enter the traffic was fast moving and it looked to me a bit like a dual carriageway.

As I approached the roundabout at this point, on my left I noticed a pathway with railings on either side. I decided to travel down the pathway, hoping for the best, as not far down this short stretch of road I would need to turn left again at yet another roundabout to bring me across the River Exe. However the pathway did not carry on far enough, and in the end I had to retreat and join the road after all. Fortunately there was a gap from the pathway to the road saving me the inconvenience of having to turn round and go back to the beginning of the pathway. I joined the busy traffic making my way towards the roundabout, and having reached this safely, I turned left on to the A 379 towards Dawlish. I managed to take some photos on the way because the road was a lot quieter and it was easy for me to stop. I continued my journey on a newly resurfaced road, relaxing a little because now there were no potholes to worry about, and I was able to take in my surroundings on the way through Kenton, Starcross, Dawlish, finally arriving at Teignmouth lifeboat station. Looking back this had indeed been a very satisfying and enjoyable journey for me.

Here I met up once again with Brenda and Brian, who had managed to collect some money for the RNLI. Teignmouth is a favourite place for Brian who had spent holidays here in the past. With the scooter on board Brian's car, the three of us returned to site, doing a small shopping top up en route before driving to the caravan.

I called the RAC out to check over the car as I was concerned about the smells which I believed were coming from the automatic clutch, when reversing, with the caravan attached. I was very relieved when the RAC found everything to be normal. Our main meal today was fish and chips, and it wasn't even Friday! Brenda and I took advantage of the disabled toilets to have a shower, but for Brian this would prove to be more difficult because once he had removed his calliper, he was no longer able to stand. Later Brenda checked the Internet but it was not working again which meant that we would have to wait until the next site and try again.

## Day 6, April 7

This morning with everything completed, we achieved the quickest hook up done by us yet. We left for Dartmouth, following the A381 through Newton Abbot, round Totnes down to Halwell, and then on to the A3122 towards Dartmouth before turning right and following signs to our next site. The car seemed okay which eased my concerns and worries for a while. We had no trouble finding the camping and caravan site at Woodland Grove, Dartmouth where we set up the caravan with a little help. It was a hot sunny day and Brenda's sister, Hazel, and her husband, Norman, who live at the top of Dartmouth, met us at the site.

After lunch Brian and I left to reach a point north of Torquay where he dropped me and the scooter off. This enabled me to travel down the A379 through Torquay, The English Riviera, where the holidaymakers enjoying the weather helped to create a relaxed atmosphere as I drove round Torbay, joined the A3022 and journeyed on through Paignton which seemed to have less of a holiday atmosphere.

I finally reached Brixham Harbour where my memories still linger on from the time that Brenda and I, Brian and his late wife Edna, had spent in a caravan holiday back in the 60s. Brian and I had driven our three wheeled trikes from Edenbridge and it had taken all day to get to Paignton. Brenda and Edna, who had travelled by train and taxi, anxiously awaited our late arrival which was due to the heavy traffic on roads which were a lot slower back then. In addition my trike had a fuel leak which meant that Brian had to siphon petrol from his tank to mine to enable me to get to the next garage and fill up. This was just the start of our adventures on that particular holiday!

Back to my journey. I drove to Brixham lifeboat station, another unmanned station, and then continued out of Brixham up the hill which the scooter coped with very well. I was naturally concerned knowing how hilly the area is but I continued on to Kingswear, descending the steep hill with tall trees on either side of the road for the most part of the journey. At the bottom of this very steep hill, I reached the lower ferry and crossed to Dartmouth where I was met by Brenda, Hazel and Sam, our dog, and we returned to the caravan site. During my absence Brenda and Hazel had sat in the sun chatting, walking the dog, doing some washing, and generally relaxing. That evening Hazel and Norman treated us to a lovely meal in the pub next to the site where we had steak and kidney pudding.

## Day 7, April 8

All up early this morning, breakfast out of the way and ready for our rendezvous. Tony, our son, had arranged with the Dartmouth Chronicle to meet us at Dartmouth lifeboat station. This is an inshore station which is fairly new to Dartmouth and ensures safety measures are in place on the river Dart. Although our mission was to visit only mainland coastal lifeboat stations and not inshore stations, we decided to make an exception in this case as Brenda's sister lives in Dartmouth, and with our caravan being sited just outside Dartmouth, this would add to our publicity.

We met Kirstan from the Dartmouth Chronicle and also the press officer for the Dartmouth RNLI at the lifeboat station. There we enjoyed a cup of tea and received a donation from a lady RNLI supporter and I was interviewed before leaving for Salcombe lifeboat station. In the meantime Brenda and Brian stayed with

Hazel, collected a little money and enjoyed an ice cream while I sped (at around 8 mph!) towards my destination.

It was a bright sunny day and I was looking forward to the journey ahead. Having stayed with Brenda's sister on many occasions I was very familiar with first part of the journey as far as Torcross. I first travelled out from Dartmouth on the back roads from the junction that leads to Dartmouth Castle and the small delightful Cafe next to it. I continued up the Hill, first with houses on either side, then rising higher now with embankments and hedgerows. I eventually passed the caravan site where we were based and on to Stoke Fleming. There were now sea views from this high plateau on my left. Then I then dropped down slightly as I passed Blackpool Sands, before climbing again with fabulous views on my left overlooking the beautiful sandy bay. I scooted on until I arrived at sea level along a four mile stretch of road passing Slapton Sands, with its freshwater wildlife sanctuary, a nature reserve, on my right.

Here at Slapton Sands tragedy occurred during the Second World War. American ships were on a training exercise when German E-boat's struck, killing many unfortunate Americans. In the car park opposite the beach stands an American tank as a memorial to those lost soldiers.

Back on my journey along another interesting part of the coast, I'm soaking up the atmosphere of freedom which riding the scooter gives me, taking in the sights and sounds as I travel, being able to stop at any time. I am living my dream and feeling so good! This was just the start of what I hoped would be one of the most memorable parts of my life. I continued along the A379 towards Kingsbridge, with more beautiful scenery, and then followed the A281 until I arrived at Salcombe lifeboat station, an unmanned station in yet another stunning location.

Brenda and Brian soon arrived to collect me for the journey back to the caravan where Brenda finished ironing and cooked the dinner before we went on to her sister's to use the Internet. Searching for sites further along the coast with electrical hook up, which of course is essential to charge the scooter batteries, at this time I wasn't fully aware that nowadays it seems all sites have electric hook ups. It had been a long time since I had last been caravanning and camping, so I found that I was slightly naive as to current facilities. At Hazel's, after using the Internet, we took advantage and had a shower before returning to the caravan late that evening.

## Day 8, April 9

The next day with breakfast over and all the jobs done, we were ready to move on. We left Dartmouth mid-morning having accepted help from members on the site to hook the caravan up to the car. I towed the caravan through Plymouth to the outskirts of Looe and on to a well-kept site on the east side at St Martin. There a man with a small tractor, while positioning the caravan for our stay, unfortunately backed it onto a slope and damaged one of the jack resting plates.

It was yet another sunny day and we were able to have our lunch outside. That afternoon my plan was to visit Plymouth lifeboat station but all did not go well. On the 10 o'clock, 11 o'clock and 12 o'clock news, Plymouth's local radio station had broadcast my anticipated arrival that day. Naturally, I attempted to reach the lifeboat station but was bitterly disappointed at having to abandon my attempt. This was because, I did not know where the lifeboat station was in the city; with hindsight I realise that I should have contacted the lifeboat station and had somebody meet me from the ferry when I crossed to Plymouth at Torpoint.

Plymouth turned out to be one of seven lifeboat stations missed on the entire trip, although we did manage to visit 150 in all. After crossing Plymouth Sound on the ferry I drove up the hill and, finding a petrol station on my right, I asked several people the way to the lifeboat station but unfortunately it seemed that even the locals didn't know they had one! After a short time I left the garage but had no idea where to go from there. With the city traffic and time against me I made the decision with great regret to abandon the day's journey. My first mistake had been to attempt to reach the lifeboat station on the same day as arriving on a new site; my second mistake had been not to pick up a map of Plymouth whilst at the garage; and my third mistake, as I've already mentioned, had been not to contact the station. I was exceedingly disappointed particularly after the announcement on Plymouth radio arranged by my son, Tony.

Finally I returned to the caravan for a fish and chips supper and spent more time on the Internet. It was a most regrettable day and it became obvious to me that moving the caravan onto a site and then trying to reach a lifeboat station all in the same day was not a very good idea. So we made it general practice with some exceptions not to do this in the future.

## Day 9, April 10

I decided not to make another attempt to visit Plymouth lifeboat station after the previous bad day and also taking into account that I had no idea how long the whole 'Scoot4Life' project would take to finish; however, with hindsight I know that there would have been time. So, to all at the lifeboat station and any members of the public who may have gone to see my arrival, I can only apologise for the poor decision I made that day.

Today was nice and hot and we were up earlier than usual. After breakfast I spent time on the Internet, looking for sites, then Brenda did the Internet banking, and after this we sorted out the caravan before leaving at 1:30pm. Brenda and Brian dropped me and the scooter off at 2:15pm and then went on to Fowey, our next lifeboat station. I travelled along the A387 until I arrived at the junction with the B3359. I now headed inland on this road to avoid what on the map looked like a spaghetti junction of back roads which would have been a headache to navigate. I followed this road until it reached the main A390 which took me down into Lostwithiel and then beyond until finally reaching the B3269 which ran down into Fowey. Fowey is an interesting place with very narrow streets and corners to negotiate. While waiting for Brenda and Brian, I enjoyed a lovely ice cream and sat looking around, the weather once again being kind to me. It's so pleasing to be travelling at no more than 8 miles an hour taking in the scenery as I go and, not being able to walk any distance, this whole journey is my walk. In Fowey we collected £15, the most yet from the public, before we returned to the caravan. Brenda phoned her Mum and Dad, I went on the

Internet again while Brian tried to sort out the TV aerial but had no luck. Greenmeanie, our webmasters, arranged for us to go onto Twitter and Brenda sent her first Tweet! We finally went to bed but Brenda was missing her TV.

## Day 10, April 11

I was up first as usual and woke the team with a cup of tea. We dressed, had our ablutions and had breakfast, then sorted out the caravan and did other bits and pieces ready for the hook up, our quickest yet. Getting better all the time!

We left the site without a problem and arrived at our new site in the early afternoon. We had booked ahead for four days at Penhale caravan and camping site near Redruth in Cornwall, a cheap site costing us £10 per night. I had a little trouble finding the entrance so we sent Brian ahead to look for it. Brenda and I waited at the side of the road for him to return with directions and when he returned it was with the site owner who showed us the way back to the site. I was facing the wrong way and had to turn round in a petrol station to follow them back to our new site. This very windy site was at a place called Lanner on top of a hillside with good views in most directions, and from here not too far away we were able to see the chimney stacks of the old tin mines. Later we were able to drive close to them and managed to take a photo or two

The owner was just completing the shower block, so Brenda decided to try it out but unfortunately, she didn't realize that to get hot water you needed to pull a switch down, which she hadn't seen. She returned to the caravan feeling not too happy and so decided to shower in the caravan. When I showered in the block later I was able to find the switch and everything was fine.

We were the only people on site for the whole four days. The owners also looked after some dogs in kennels which were not that far from our caravan, but far enough not to cause us any problems. The kennels seem to be their main source of income. Brian and I spent some time successfully trying to get the TV working using the free sat dish, which we mounted on my tripod. Once we were settled and after lunch, we went to Tesco in Redruth to stock up with supplies. Returning to the caravan, we tried to get on the Internet without any luck but at least we could watch the television.

## Day 11, April 12

The day started off with a pleasant sunny morning and the wind had dropped nicely. After breakfast we made rolls for lunch to take to Falmouth. With lunch over, I left on my way to the Lizard on the A39 turning off at the junction with the A394 which I followed to Flambards and from there I took the A3083 heading towards Lizard Point. Having left the main road, taking in my surroundings as I went, I found this the most pleasant part of my journey. I still needed to keep my eye on the road, especially for potholes which could potentially cause a puncture or even throw the scooter off course. Listening to the sound of the scooter is a kind of comfort to me, especially from time to time when walls and other solid objects would echo its sound as I passed by.

Brenda and Brian drove to Mullion Cove where they took some photos, Brenda telling me later how nice the Cove was. They passed me in the car on their way to the Lizard and I finally arrived some three hours later, after a journey of approximately twenty-three miles passing through some fantastic countryside on the way.

I eventually found the lifeboat station after first discovering the previous one, built some years ago, and now disused. The weather stayed good all day making this place look like a picture postcard and we managed to take some beautiful photos of the area. To reach the lifeboat station meant first opening the metal gate across the driveway leading to the station, although from this point the station was not in view. I travelled on and around a corner came to an area much like a building site where I found three RNLI crew members. I had a chat with them and they explained the reason for the work which was going on, which was the construction of a brand new lifeboat station. There had been several lifeboat stations at the Lizard over time; the first was built in 1859 at Polpeor Cove, the second, larger station was built in 1885 lower down in the Cove, and the final station at the Cove was completed in 1914. In 1867 RNLI had built an additional lifeboat station at Cadgwith, a fishing village on the East side the Lizard, which remained in service until 1963 when the stations were merged with the Lizard's Kilcobben Cove station. The first station was opened in July 1961 and was the result of amalgamating the two former lifeboat stations at Polpeor Cove and Cadgwith. In 2010 the original station was demolished so, on my arrival in 2011, I was witnessing the construction of a brand new station which opened on May 5th 2012 as the RNLI constantly upgrade their stations to meet modern demands.

As usual the crew invited us for coffee but at this time neither Brenda nor Brian were with me as they were still wandering around

View on the Lizard.

this beautiful place, taking photos. I explained this to the guys and went off to look for them; however it wasn't long before I returned having not managed to find them. Because of this I declined the offer of coffee, said my goodbyes and went to find the other two. Once together again, we eventually visited the village and had a look round. We found a shop selling Cornish pasties at the back of someone's house and ordered three for lunch for the next day. This is definitely an area in the country I will put on my wish list of places to return to in the future. Then we went back to the caravan where we managed to persuade Brian to cook our dinner.

## Day 12, April 13

Brian cooked breakfast. He enjoys his fry-ups in the morning but we persuaded him that it might be a good idea to have cereals or toast for breakfast now and again. Brenda's sister, Hazel, phoned us for the usual catch up. We managed to get on the Internet and booked three days ahead, Friday, Saturday and Sunday at a cost of between £60 & £70 at a site near Bude. Brenda did a Tweet, and, to our surprise later on in the journey, we discovered that one of our followers just happened to be Stephen Fry. Also Tony phoned. It's so surprising how long all these little things take and although I was often up around 8:30 in the morning we never seemed to get away very early each day. It was almost like a military operation working out exactly what we were going to do for that particular day.

We drove to Penzance through pouring rain and strong winds and got to the point that I had picked to start the scooter run for that day. My first stop was an hour away, at Sennen Cove, just north of Lands End. In 1851 the RNLI had built a boathouse at the top of the beach, but after a few changes over time, in 2001 the roof was removed and a new one installed ready to receive the faster Tamer class boat. Over the years the crews have received several silver and bronze medals for their bravery. We met a crew member in the lifeboat station who made us a nice hot cup of tea, which went well with the pasties we had bought for our lunch the day before. The man kindly phoned ahead to advise the lifeboat station at St Ives that we were on our way.

I left Sennen Cove and crossed the moors in very poor conditions, visibility was really bad in the misty rain. This was just the first of a few bad days that we were to experience with the weather. Brenda and Brian had stopped in a lay-by to check on my progress as I moved on to my destination for the day. Driving carefully in these unfavourable conditions, I followed B3306 along the coast, arriving at St Ives some two hours later but there was nobody on the RNLI station despite the phone call.

We loaded the scooter into Brian's car and returned to the caravan for a nice hot cooked dinner, followed by hot showers to end a miserable day. I'm sure the scenery along this part of the coast would have been great if the weather had stayed kind to us but there were still plenty of beautiful runs in the days and weeks ahead for us. Before we retired for the night, Brenda managed to do some more work on the laptop writing updates which kept us in touch with family and friends back at home.

## Day 13, April 14

By morning the wind had dropped and the rain had stopped, but it was still cloudy although much milder. After breakfast, leaving the caravan late morning, we set off for the next drop off point on the way to St Agnes lifeboat station. We drove along the A30 to the end of the dual carriageway at a place called Three Burrows, and here I started my journey on the B3277, a short run of roughly two miles. There was no one at this station and, after meeting up with Brenda and Brian, we had lunch. St Agnes looked like a really nice place, with lots of surfing going on. After lunch, Brenda and Brian went ahead to Newquay and I set off on the B3285, scooting along the coast road enjoying the relatively fine weather which we were now experiencing. At Perranporth where I joined the A3075 the road turns inland. The journey from St Agnes to Newquay took approximately two hours, a pretty but uneventful journey.

It took me some time to find the others. The first lifeboat station I found had been used for over one hundred years but was now no longer in use, so the search was on for the one used today. Eventually I found the station tucked away down the hill in the harbour. 'Not a bad place to put a lifeboat station,' I thought to myself! It couldn't have been in a more obvious place. This was another unmanned station so we decided to have a look round the town as it had been many years since I last visited Newquay. We took a few photos before returning to the caravan where we prepared sweet-and-sour chicken and rice for our main meal of the day.

## Day 14, April 15

We were up and off the site by mid morning. I towed the caravan to a site near Bude, Widemouth Fields Caravan & Camping Park, which has an entrance from a lay-by. We arrived around lunchtime and settled the caravan on our pitch which was level and very easy to position the caravan on. If only all sites were like this! We connected the usual utilities and then had lunch. Brenda sorted out the washing while I was going over the next day's plans. Then we went to reception where there were very chatty and friendly people who helped us to book our next two sites. After this we drove to Bude where we used the ATM, filled the cars with fuel and did our shopping for the next three days. We also enjoyed a fish and chip supper before returning back to the caravan for the evening. No TV reception. Sorry, Bren!

## Day 15, April 16

We were all up by 8:30am this morning but didn't get going until three hours later, a familiar start to the day. Brenda and Brian drove to Padstow, dropping me off on the A39 near the junction with the A395. From there I headed south towards Wadebridge, after travelling down this major road, the A39, without any problems. I drove through Wadebridge and turned right onto the A389 to complete the first stage of a two lifeboat station run. It had been a nice smooth journey so far and the weather once again was on my side. I couldn't quite believe how dry it had been for us so far, although travelling at only eight miles per hour, I still felt cold as I moved through the air.

When Brenda and Brian arrived at Padstow they discovered that the lifeboat station had been closed and a new one, which was only accessible at the weekend opened, on what was known as The Rock. Subsequently I learnt from the Internet that a lifeboat station had been initially established in Padstow, situated on the western side of the River Camel, directly opposite the village of Rock on the eastern side. The station was established in 1825 but was not fully taken over by the RNLI until 1856. The current lifeboat station is now located at Mother Ivey's Bay on Trevose Head. It was re-sited from Hawkers Cove in 1967 due to the river silting up and now means that the Tamer class lifeboat can be launched into deep water no matter what the state of the tide. There is also a D class inshore boat at the station.

Brenda and Brian waited an hour and a half to two hours in Padstow for me to arrive. Learning about the situation we were disappointed for this meant missing another station but we went off to drown our sorrows in yet more coffee at a nearby café. While Brenda and Brian were waiting for me, they had managed to collect £15 in Brian's tin which helped to ease our disappointment. We had lunch and then I set off for Port Isaac.

I doubled back to Weybridge where I picked up the B3314, and as I travelled through some of Cornwall's wonderful countryside I felt unbelievably lucky in being able to do this project with the help of so many friends and family. I eventually found Brenda and Brian at Port Isaac where they had met two people who had seen us on Meridian television. We went down to the harbour and found the unmanned lifeboat station, which is positioned across the road from the beach with steep hills on either side of the small harbour as seen on TV. There in a shop window was a picture of Martin Clunes, who plays the leading role in Doc Martin,

Eventually we returned to the car, which was in a car park quite some distance away from the harbour on the right when facing the sea, and we returned to the caravan for dinner. Brenda sorted out the washing as well as doing the ironing on the table since we had no ironing board. In the early hours of the morning, around 4am, I awoke and realized that we had not connected the batteries to recharge. which would mean a late start for the next day's stations. By now we had an established routine and it was Brian's job to connect the batteries for charging; somehow this time it had slipped his memory, and mine!

## Day 16, April 17

I woke first as usual to a hot morning and managed to get Brian out of bed by 7 am to connect the batteries and make sure we had the power needed for the day, another two target day. Because of the late start, Brian cooked a lovely fry up to set us up for the day ahead and for a change we had showers in the morning. Brenda did some hand washing and other chores, before we finally left the site, on our way to Bude lifeboat station. There we had a quick chat with a lifeboat volunteer before leaving for Clovelly. My journey along the A39 from Bude was approximately ten miles which took me about one and a half hours, and, although not an unpleasant ride, it was not very interesting travelling along the main road.

When I reached Clovelly, Brenda and Brian went down to the harbour as there was no access available for the scooter, just lots of steps, while I waited with Sam until their return. Brenda was able to take some photos of the harbour which I had visited many years ago when I had been taken down by Land Rover. It is one of those harbours not to miss.

Brenda and Brian drove on to Appledore where luckily they met one of the volunteers and told him about our project, while I was still on route. He phoned their press officer and coxswain, and so, when I finally arrived, I was met by a large number of the crew. I hadn't been quite sure exactly where the lifeboat station was but when Brenda contacted me on my mobile, I could give her my location, which enabled them to send a crew member on a motorbike to show me the way. I had been following the main route into Appledore and I was on a road parallel to the lifeboat station, higher up the hill roughly behind the station. Meanwhile the crew had opened up the station and pulled the inshore lifeboat out onto the slipway. We gathered around with the crew in front of the boat so that the press officer could take photos of our arrival and these appeared on their website and in the North Devon Chronicle. This was the first time that a large number of crew had specially turned out to meet us and it gave us a little extra boost. As I have mentioned before many of the lifeboat stations are unmanned, although we do have contact with people working in the RNLI shops, where the stations may have one. Appledore RNLI station has an all-weather Tamer class and an inshore B class Atlantic Over its 180 year history the crews have received thirty-one awards for gallantry.

By now it was late afternoon turning early evening but the sun was still shining gloriously and it was a lovely feeling; I think all of us ended up with a warm glow inside, just like the sun shining and reflecting on the sea in front of us. What a great day it had turned out to be! We drove back to the caravan for a late dinner having soaked up the atmosphere of our experience with the crew at Appledore lifeboat station. Thanks to them!

I must add that unbeknown to us at the same time back home there was a fund-raising evening going on in our local pub, the Old Eden. There they had arranged a race night to raise funds for the RNLI on our behalf. Our thanks go to Linda and Roger and all those people involved in this event.

## Day 17, April 18

We left the site late morning after preparing the caravan for a long journey of approximately 120 miles to the next site at Weston super Mare. By doing this, it meant missing out the Ilfracombe lifeboat station, but this was because we were unable to find a suitable site for our needs bearing in mind that we were travelling with Sam, our pet dog. There will be more about him in the days ahead. Some sites, according to the Caravanning Handbook, would not take a dog and this proved to be a minor headache throughout the journey. We were members of the Camping and Caravanning Club and the Caravan Club. We also had a book of independent caravan sites but in the end it was mostly the two books just mentioned which we used. On the way to the Weston super Mare site, we pulled into a lay-by and made ourselves tea and sandwiches for lunch. After arriving at the new site, once all the utilities were connected/done, we set off to get money for fuel and shopping, returning to the caravan, where Brian cooked the evening meal. Later that evening we were able to Skype with Jenny, a friend of ours, and our son Tony, luckily having a reasonable Internet connection for a change.

# Day 18, April 19

Before we left for the day's journey ahead, I reflected on how long it took us to organise ourselves and to prepare for each day and how, with most of the morning often already gone, we still managed to achieve our goals! Then I phoned my sister Val to arrange to meet up the next day with her and her husband John, as they lived not too far away in Bridgwater.

After settling into our next caravan site, which was at West End Farm, Burnham-on-Sea, we sat and enjoyed our lunch in the warm sun by the sea. Our plan on leaving the site was to travel the long way back to Minehead Lifeboat station where, after dropping me off, Brenda and Brian would go on to Watchet. In the picture Brenda is on the harbour-side by the statue commemorating the poem *The Rime of the Ancient Mariner* by Samuel Taylor Coleridge. They spent an hour and a half looking around the attractive harbour and managed to collect a small amount of money. In 1944 Watchet Lifeboat station was closed in favour of Minehead with its new power boat, which would be able to cover the Watchet area. Although I was scooting some twenty-seven miles from Minehead back to Burnham-on-Sea on the A39, passing Dunster Castle and Gardens (National Trust), a place we intended to come back to, I took a slight detour to join them briefly.

Statue commemorating the poem *The Rime of the Ancient Mariner* by
Samuel Taylor Coleridge

Back on the what I thought was the A39, due to a lack of
concentration, I found myself on the A358! Luckily for me I soon
arrived at a junction and in a field just through a gate next to the
road a farmer was busy working and so it wasn't long before I was
helped back onto the correct route. I had left Brenda and Brian for
a long journey and it was three hours and forty minutes before I
met up with them again. The tricky bit for me was getting round
Bridgwater, trying to avoid the dual carriageway; however there
was a path running alongside the carriageway the whole length
of the drive and I managed to use that to bypass the bypass, so
to speak! The scooter managed the ups and downs of the road

so, apart from Bridgwater, this was yet another reasonably good journey. It is not always possible to take in my surroundings as I scoot along because I need to concentrate on the road ahead, not only for the traffic, but for those dreadful potholes. Although it had been a long journey, I had very much enjoyed it; for me it was like walking the coast at twice the speed of an average walker.

After our evening meal, we managed to access the Internet and were able to Skype our friends and family.

# Day 19, April 20

We awoke to a lovely hot morning and had boiled eggs and toast for breakfast setting us up for the day ahead. Brenda's sister, Hazel, phoned, wanting to know where we were and how we were getting on, Everyone always wanted to know our whereabouts and how things were going and it was good to be able to keep in contact with friends and family during the trip using modern technology. There were also other interested parties who were following our progress. Before leaving Burnham-on-Sea we met my sister Val and her husband John at the RNLI shop just of the High Street leading to Pier Street and Old Station approach and enjoyed a chat with them. My only regret was not being able to visit them at their house, but I was feeling under pressure not knowing how long the entire project would take, and so didn't allow myself that luxury. We bought sandwiches from a shop nearby and had our lunch with them, before I left for Weston-super-Mare, a short journey of around six miles.

Along the B3140, turning left on the A38 for a short stretch before coming onto the A 370, which took me into Western-super-Mare and along the very clean promenade with the new pier standing proudly in the sea. Once again it was an uneventful but warm journey and Brenda and Brian were waiting at the lifeboat gift shop having already been served with cups of tea by the people running the shop. The Lifeboat Station, now just off Knightstone Road overlooking Marine Lake replaces the one on the derelict pier damaged by past storms, and was unmanned on our arrival.

I was immediately made very welcome with a cuppa for myself and we stayed in Western-super-Mare until late afternoon. Since it was still hot and sunny we took the opportunity to collect money for the RNLI by staying close to the lifeboat station on the promenade with some success. Note the Lifeboat Teddy Bear and the tall flag pole in this picture.

Raising money in Western-super-Mare.

We eventually returned to the caravan for dinner and later that evening we were once again updating emails, before showering, and retiring to bed. The next day we would be crossing the River Severn into South Wales, the next stage of what was turning out to be a successful first part of the project. I felt good about what lay ahead.

# CHAPTER EIGHT

# Wales

### Day 20, April 21

Another moving day full of excitement! With all the utilities disconnected and put in their appropriate places, we hooked up, and left for South Wales and our next site which was Caemawr Farm, Furnace, Llanelli between Gorseinon and Barry Port.

We arrived at the caravan site by 1 o'clock, the cost here was £12 per night. My car wasn't happy reversing up a slight hill but fortunately a fellow caravanner saw us struggling and offered to help. We unhitched the caravan, but forgot to disconnect the emergency brake cable which was connected to the tow bar and the caravan brakes. As I drove away the cable snapped. Once again, fortunately for us, on this small site were a group of caravanners, one of whom repaired caravans for a living, and for just £10 he fixed a new cable for us. Our helper then hitched his car to our caravan successfully reversed it into position. We couldn't have had better luck or been more thankful!

Eventually we had our lunch sitting in the sun – can you believe it – before heading off into Llanelli for shopping, fuel, etc. We returned for our evening meal and afterwards managed to do some Internet banking but we still couldn't get TV in our caravan.

# Day 21, April 22

Our simple breakfast this Good Friday morning consisted of hot cross buns which was very enjoyable. We left late morning to drive to Barry Docks a journey of some fifty miles South East from the caravan. Here, once again, there was nobody on site, this station sits on the East side of the Barry Island pleasure park in the outer harbour, from here I set off on the scooter heading for the next lifeboat station, at Atlantic College. By now it was raining and although a little unpleasant it wasn't too far to ride. I was managing to stay dry in my wet gear while listening to the sound of the scooter's wheels as I travelled on the wet road surface. Passing by Cardiff Airport, I seemed to be the only one on the road and now the weather was changing and it became both sunny and cloudy, but pleasantly warm. I continued my journey along the B4265 skirting around the southern edge of the small village of St Athan and the nearby Royal Air Force station, and then moving on to skirt around the northern edge of Llantwit Major a much bigger built up area.

Here I met up with Brenda and Brian who had arrived at Atlantic College lifeboat station to find there was absolutely nobody about and the College was closed, this station was one of the first experimental inshore stations opened in 1963, but closed in 2013 and is now used for training beach Lifeguards, after their brief visit they turned around, and headed back to meet me. We decided it was pointless for me to make that trip myself.

The rain had returned, and leaving Llantwit Major, I set off for Porthcawl lifeboat station, I kept to the same road B4265 which took me away from the coast and towards a tiny place called Wick, heading for St Brides Major. The journey was mostly void of traffic again, which made it a much more pleasant run for me. I followed the road to Bridgend where I joined the A473 and I followed this until it brought me to my target road the A4106, which took me down to Porthcawl.

At the Lifeboat Station, which is situated next to the National Coast watch tower on the promenade overlooking jagged rocks at the water's edge, again when I finally arrived there was nobody on site, apart from Brenda and Brian. We loaded the scooter into Brian's car and drove on to Port Talbot, for fish and chips, before returning to the caravan.

## Day 22, April 23

Today was an uneventful day. We decided to catch up on more chores. Brian went to get a haircut, Brenda and I went to buy an aerial connection in the hope we could get the TV working, and we returned to the caravan for lunch outside as it was another sunny day – our luck with the weather seemed to be holding. We left the site to find the nearby lifeboat station at Barry Port, on the jetty leading out to the Lighthouse with its sandy beaches on either side. Having done that the search was on for coffee, before exploring our surroundings. Barry Port seemed a pleasant sort of place to spend an afternoon. This picturesque marina with its pleasure craft and tourists now dominated the once busy port used for shipping coal from the nearby pits.

We returned to caravan for dinner, and spent the evening sending off our weekly emails etc, before retiring to bed.

## Day 23, April 24

Lots of texts arrived this morning from everyone wishing us a Happy Easter. We left the caravan behind and drove to Horton and then Port Eynon which is situated west of Swansea on the Gower Peninsula. When we arrived we just could not find the lifeboat station, so I made the decision to leave Brenda and Brian and make my way to the Mumbles. Later they found the lifeboat station at Port Eynon down a dead end road from the village of Horton.

The route to the Mumbles was going to be a long scoot, following back roads leading to the A4118 and eventually arriving on the B4436. I travelled through some great countryside finally arriving at Black Pill by the sea where I turned right and travelled down the long ride towards my destination. What a fantastic ride! This trip to The Mumbles was one of my favourites. It was a very long journey, as mentioned, with lovely weather for me to enjoy. There were one or two obstacles on the journey namely cattle grids, which the scooter couldn't cross. So I had to go through the side gates which were not easy for me to open because they were rarely used and they dragged along the ground with all the greenery and rubbish which had accumulated in front of them. I had my doubts for a while about one of the gates in particular as to whether I would be able to open it; however, as the saying goes 'Where there's a will there's a way' and with a great effort I did get through.

On my journey to the station, I spent four and a half hours on the scooter but I'm not complaining as it was such a great ride. My experience on the scooter just gets better and better. I had arrived at The Mumbles ahead of Brenda and Brian and managed to make contact with two people connected to the lifeboat station via the people in the shop. When Brenda and Brian arrived, they came outside and we all posed for photographs. The Mumbles promenade is about five miles long and the Lifeboat Station perches at the end. It is a place that is well worth a visit. A lifeboat station known as the Swansea lifeboat station was first opened in 1835, then the RNLI took it over and moved it to The Mumbles in 1866, and it became known as The Mumbles lifeboat station in 1904.

We eventually loaded the scooter into Brian's car, and returned to the caravan for showers, etc. During the night Sam, our pet dog, couldn't settle for two and a half hours, we thought he may have had some sort of tummy ache, and wondered what he might have eaten.

## Day 24, April 25

Thankfully Sam had recovered his usual high spirits by this morning and so we decided to have breakfast outside, taking every advantage of the weather and the magnificent views across the Gower Peninsula. Then I set off to travel to Barry Port some 6 miles away. The owners of the site were very friendly people who lived in a typical farmhouse close by nestling neatly in with the surrounding countryside. As I passed their house I stopped for a chat with them they told me that there was a cycle track I could use to travel all the way to my destination. This had originally been a railway track, but was now a cycle route. I decided to try it out. I joined the track not far from the farm and started my journey along this attractive trail surrounded by trees and fields but it wasn't long before I came across a barrier which would only allow cyclists through. I could go no further and I had no choice but to return to a point where I could get back onto the road. Once there I took the A484 and then turned left onto the B4311 which ran parallel with the beach, until arriving at Burry Port where I met up with Brenda and Brian.

With nobody at the lifeboat station, it didn't take us long to decide to go and find a coffee. It was such a pleasant day that we had a walk/scoot round after coffee. Brenda walked Sam, Brian and I scooted, we all took photos overlooking the sandy beach and the jetty with the Lighthouse at the end We had lunch sitting close to the beach.

We then left to travel to a place called Ferryside where we had been told there was a RNLI lifeboat station which did not appear on our map. We decided to check it out but when we arrived we discovered it was called St. John's and had been taken over from RNLI by the locals who felt that there should still be a lifeboat station at this point. The RNLI in 1960 transferred the Station to Angle in Pembrokeshire and the Station was close. We stayed for a while overlooking the estuary and the railway line. Later returning to the caravan and sitting out in the field with a cup of tea, while again admiring the scenery from the high point overlooking the Bristol Channel and the Gower. Later we tried the TV but with no luck. We were using a satellite dish beside the caravan which was attached to my camera tripod. It had worked well before, but unfortunately the wind caught it and over it went breaking the dish fittings. I should have weighted the tripod as I would have done if I had mounted a camera on it in windy conditions.

## Day 25, April 26

On the move again. Breakfast finished, the caravan sorted and were on our way. We travelled some fifty-seven miles to the little haven Haverfordwest in Pembrokeshire to a really nice site. We settled the caravan, connected all the usual utilities and then went shopping, stopping in the town for lunch before returning to site. Washing also needed to be done whenever the opportunity arose because we never knew what would be available at the next site, or whether we would need to go into the nearest town to find a launderette. That afternoon It rained for about two hours and so I took the opportunity to scan the map for future caravan sites ready for or our next move, using the two club books. After dinner, we went on a ride to a place called Dale Point which overlooked the mouth of the Milford Haven estuary, a busy shipping channel leading to Pembroke docks. Once again we overlooked a beautiful part of South Wales with Great Castle Head in the distance.

We returned to Little Haven Caravan site later for bed. Brenda had left the washing to dry overnight in the shower room and I was hoping I wouldn't need to go to the loo during the night and have to manoeuvre round Brenda's secret mantrap!

# Day 26, April 27

A clear blue sky this morning – another good weather day ahead. We had a text message from our son Terry to say all ok. Tony phoned to tell us he had managed to contact Radio Wales so they could interview me by my mobile phone. I managed to get through to them and had a chat explaining all about the project. Interview over, we all left in Brian's car to go to Angle lifeboat station where we parked Brian's car, unloaded the scooter, and explored the village.

We came across the local village hall, serving light refreshments to raise money for local charities and we went in and enjoyed the coffee and cake which was on offer. We left there to find the lifeboat station. Brenda and I were surprised to find a new station had been built but we didn't meet any crew there although Brenda walked around to see if she could find anyone. Back in June 2009, Brenda and I had had a holiday in Pembrokeshire and had visited this area, at which time the lifeboat station was a rather large shed type construction. The new station now stands much closer to the water's edge than before. At 1pm I left Brenda and Brian at Angle sitting in a pub garden overlooking this quiet and small part of the river estuary. I may have missed a pint but more than made up for it by enjoying my journey to Tenby, anticipating many more delightful rides ahead. During our first six weeks on the road, although occasionally cold, it had turned out to be sunny with little rain to speak of. So far into the project, we could not have hoped for a better start which helped us settle into a routine for the rest of the project. I left Angle for Tenby, a much busier place at the end of the day to collect more donations for the RNLI.

Travelling away from Angle, I made my way along the B4320 towards Pembroke overlooking the shipping route into the docks on my left. Clear blue skies gave me great views and there were no hedgerows to interfere. For almost thirty years the Royal Air Force had been based at Pembroke Dock. During 1943, when it was home to Sunderland flying boats, it was said to be the largest operational base for flying boats in the world. During the Second World War Pembroke Dock was a major target for the Luftwaffe and on Monday 19th August 1940 a Luftwaffe bomber flew up the estuary and bombed a series of oil tanks sited at Pennar. The oil-fuelled fire that followed allegedly raged for 18 days and was said to be the largest UK fire since the Great Fire of London.

I arrived mid-afternoon in Tenby, thoroughly enjoying the ride and helped by a nice warm sunny day. Journey's end, I met up with Brenda and Brian in Tenby, we went on to the lifeboat station and met the coxswain who soon arranged for photos to be taken of us for their publicity. Tenby lifeboat station has operated for over 150 years and now has an all-weather lifeboat and an inshore D class lifeboat. It was the first Station to receive the new slipway-launched Tamer class lifeboat. The third lifeboat station built at Tenby was established 1852 by shipwrecked fishermen and the Mariners Royal Benevolent Society. Since 1854 when the RNLI took over the station, five bronze medals and ten silver medals have been awarded to crew members. We later wandered around Tenby before leaving late in the afternoon, with the weather still hot. It must be said Tenby is a great place to visit.

We returned to the caravan for dinner. To give you an insight into our domestic arrangements, Brian had one end of the caravan where his bed was permanently set up, Brenda and I used the living area for our bed. Obviously this had to be put together on a daily basis before we could settle down for the night. Sam slept in his bed on the floor beside us and occasionally he would creep up into our bed for comfort and warmth during the night.

## Day 27, April 28

Today was Brenda's mother's 88th birthday and both our boys phoned us this morning, It's always nice to hear from them when you're far from home. Brian cooked us mackerel for breakfast, one of my favourites and Brenda phoned her mother wishing her happy birthday from us all. We left site in the morning to go to Little and Broad Haven lifeboat station, where on our arrival at the shop we received £5 for the RNLI from the volunteer running the shop. After a short conversation here, I left at midday for St Davids.

I travelled along, unclassified roads, slightly inland at first, then back towards the coast overlooking Newgate Sands before reaching the A487, which took me to St Davids with its fine Cathedral and the nearby ruins of St David's Bishops Palace. While looking around the Cathedral I was approached by a male and female couple, who had noticed my RNLI stickers and the flag on the scooter, They introduced themselves to me as crew members of the RNLI and that later I would probably meet them at their lifeboat station further up the coast. Sure enough this is exactly what happened. After being pointed in the right direction, I continued my journey along the B4583 to St Davids Head arriving there some two hours or so later. Brenda and Brian had arrived earlier and Brenda had walked Sam around the coast path with its stunning views. When

St Davids lifeboat station and the wonderful views of the Welsh coast.

I arrived, I was greeted by the coxswain, who came up from the lifeboat station via a great number of steps; he shook my hand and we talked about the project before he returned to the station. We sat at the top of the stairs having lunch, as people were coming up and going down to the boat for bird watching trips to Ramsey Island. Incidentally they offered to take the three of us for half price but the project came first and, at this time, I was still unsure as to how long it would take us to finish the project. With hindsight we should have accepted their offer, despite having to tackle the steps down to the boat and back after the trip. I would definitely like to go on that trip to the island in the future, but for now it will remain at the back of my mind. Nevertheless we managed to collect £19 from passers by and Brian managed to lose a sandwich to somebody's hungry dog! After all the excitement and the look on Brian's face, I left mid afternoon for Fishguard.

I travelled along the A487 using the most direct route instead of roads closer to the coast which would have been a far more attractive journey, but from a navigational point of view the direct route was so much easier. Meeting up with Brenda and Brian, we had a coffee from a mobile canteen in the car park overlooking Fishguard Bay. In order to find the lifeboat station, we first made our way to the railway station, behind which was the lifeboat station. There we were met by several crew members and, guess what, had another coffee and a good long chat with them as we sat in the sun outside the lifeboat station, our last one for that day. Fishguard lifeboat station was taken over by the RNLI in 1855 and over the years, due to the crews' bravery, it had been awarded bronze and silver medals. In 1921 the then coxswain, John Howells, received a gold medal for his bravery and in 2003 coxswain Francis George was awarded an MBE by the Queen. Returning to the caravan, I reflected on a great day for me on the scooter on yet another sunny reasonably warm day, having managed to raise more money for the RNLI.

## Day 28, April 29

Well I have to say it again, it is a lovely warm sunny day. This was getting too good to be true and my words must be getting boring, keeping on mentioning the glorious weather we were experiencing. After we left the site, we noticed there was hardly any traffic probably due to the fact it was William and Kate's wedding day, but for us it was just another moving day, driving 74 miles to Aberystwyth. We arrived at our chosen site, Midfield Caravan Park, at lunchtime, but there was no sign of Brian. We found the owner of the site having lunch, but she was not best pleased to be disturbed, as one could tell from her attitude. She told us we could put the caravan wherever we liked on one of the designated positions but unfortunately for us the site was on a hill and, as I attempted to back the caravan into position, my car was shuddering and stalling and emitting a horrible smell from the engine. I struggled for some time with this problem which kept re-occurring as I tried to back the caravan into position. Brian had still not returned to site and now we badly needed his help. I decided to try backing up further along the site, but the car was still stalling. This time there was no help from anybody on site. We rested the car for a while before trying again later. Brenda shed her first few tears over our problem, and I was beginning to think this might be the end of the trip but after a while I managed to get the caravan into a position enabling us to connect to the electricity supply. I may have panicked a little because I phoned John, the caravan owner, telling him of our current situation, and he reassured me by saying that one of his employees would come and sort out any problems with the caravan. I suppose I just needed to unburden my worries at this time and I'm extremely glad that I never had to call on his help, as I phoned the RAC and they came out to us on site to check the car. The RAC man drove the car up and down the drive on the site and he was convinced there was nothing wrong with it, but to be absolutely sure, he took the car out onto the road to test it. It was all good news on his return and he suggested that the ram brake on the caravan might have been the cause of part of the problem, so he used a grease gun on the ram break. Then he hooked the caravan onto the car and drove it to and fro, and declared that we could carry on, and not have to worry. During all this Brenda was also worried that we didn't have much fuel left in the tank although I explained that just down the road, perhaps a mile away, there was a petrol station, but on hearing our conversation the RAC man poured some diesel from a can he was carrying in his van, into our tank, announcing this was his donation toward our project, (and if you're the same man reading this story, thank you once again and for your reassurance, kindness and for lifting our spirits.)

When Brian finally arrived he told us that he had gone for lunch and coffee at a café. We had to explain to him that he was part of a team and that we needed him with us when we settled the caravan on a site. After calming down we received a call from my sister-in-law Angie to tell us that her daughter was in hospital with her liver not functioning properly, a worrying time for the family. My sister Ann phoned for a catch up and so we were able to tell her about all the day's woes. It had been one hell of a day!

## Day 29, April 30

After yesterday, things could only get better. We left the site late this morning, on the hunt to find a launderette. Having found one it meant waiting an hour for the washing to finish, so Brenda and I decided to cross the road to a pub for a drink. In the meantime, Brian had gone on to Devil's Bridge to have a ride on the scenic railway. After completing our washing expedition, Brenda and I returned to the caravan with the washing and then left for Devil's Bridge to meet with Brian, and see him off. We stayed on to take some photos on a very warm day, 23°. before returning to the caravan for salad outside in the sun, later back on the laptop to catch up with emails, etc.

## Day 30, May 1

Wow, what a night! It felt as though there were gale force winds blowing all night long waking both Brenda and me several times. Brenda was seriously concerned that the caravan might be blown over. However by morning the wind had eased slightly and we awoke to a bright sunny day. After breakfast we left site to go back down the coast to Cardigan lifeboat station where we met a couple of crew members. The first lifeboat station was established there in 1849 and by 1850 it had been taken over by the RNLI. It had two inshore boats a class B. and class D. We had a nice long chat with them before I left for Newquay. My journey took me along the A 487 before turning left onto the A486. The weather was still sunny but very windy so it was head down to get to Newquay lifeboat station. Because of the wind my journey was not too comfortable but otherwise uneventful. Brenda and Brian arrived there before me and talked with the lady in the shop who had heard of our journey around the UK. I arrived half an hour earlier than expected. Then we all had the inevitable ice cream, loaded the car with the scooter and returned to the caravan. We cooked dinner, caught up with the weekly emails and Skyped. Back home everyone was celebrating Brenda's mother's birthday,

## Day 31, May 2

This was another night with what felt like gale force winds keeping Brenda awake until about 3:30am. When we finally awoke for breakfast the wind was still strong but it was sunny with a beautiful blue sky. We drove to Aberystwyth lifeboat station where we unloaded the scooter. This was noticed by a lady volunteer lifeboat crew member who was just leaving the station to collect her mother and take her shopping. She asked about the RNLI flag which was now firmly attached to the scooter. Hearing about our project she kindly volunteered to open the up lifeboat station and allow us to look round. The boathouse sheltered two inshore boats, B-822 Spirit of Friendship and an Atlantic A-78. In May 1963 Aberystwyth was the first lifeboat station to be equipped with an inshore lifeboat and the first rescue took place on June 3rd.

After our visit I set off for Borth lifeboat station. I travelled along the B4572 coastal road, with excellent views across Cardigan Bay, and downhill into Borth. Suddenly a gust of wind caught my hat and blew it off behind me. I pulled over to the side of the road to allow the traffic to pass and allow me to go back and rescue it. Suddenly I was tapped on the shoulder by a young lady with my hat in her hand. It turned out to that she had seen what happened from the car following behind me. She realised why I had stopped and had kindly also stopped to retrieve my hat, which was much appreciated. When I finally arrived at the station Brenda and Brian were already there waiting for me. They had told the people in the shop about my planned arrival that very windy day and they greeted us with a hot cup of coffee which we had with our lunch on the sheltered side of the lifeboat station.

Brenda and Brian then drove around the 22 miles of estuaries to reach Barmouth lifeboat station while I left to do the journey on the scooter. However the wind was extremely strong and very cold. Although I had five layers of clothing on, the cold seemed to penetrate right through to my core and was spoiling what I thought would have been a great ride. I grappled with my conscience knowing that I would be letting myself down but finally decided to abort my journey. I found a convenient place to stop and, after phoning, wait for Brenda and Brian to return and pick me up. I had to wait about half an hour for them to return before I could get away from the cold. This turned out to be one of the few times on the entire trip when I had to make such a painful decision. On our way back to the caravan we picked up pasties and chips for dinner. It was a day that ended in disappointment for me.

## Day 32, May 3

We awoke to a warm sunny morning. It was still windy but not as bad as the day before. After sorting out the utilities and hooking up the caravan we left late morning to travel the 62 miles to our next site at Tyddyn Madyn Golan Garr, Dolbenmaen, Gwynedd. On arrival we contacted the owner who offered to position the caravan for us as the site was on a slight hill. He positioned the caravan at the lower end of the site, on a grassy patch, with a few other caravans. The occupants there made us welcome. On our journey to the site we had passed some major road works where a new roundabout was part of the work in progress. After settling the caravan and connecting the utilities we all drove to the local shopping centre to buy a TV aerial and chemicals for the toilet. We then went on to Tesco's for more shopping. That evening we had chicken salad sitting in the warm sunshine outside the caravan. On our way to the site we noticed it was not too far from Portmeirion so, after the meal, we drove there only to find it closed for the day. This is a place we had never visited but hope to return there sometime in the future. Then we returned to the caravan and settled down for the night.

## Day 33, May 4

We had such good luck with the weather, with a lovely sunny start to the day again. The previous day Brenda had done our washing as soon as we arrived on site and had put it on the dryer to air overnight. Tony phoned to say that he was watching a programme on TV about Barmouth and mentioned how nice it looked.

I planned to travel on my own there and back for my own peace of mind after my recent failure. Brian dropped me off at the junction of the A487 and the A4085 at the beginning of a toll road (incidentally, no toll to pay) at a place called Penrhyndeudraeth. I travelled south and following the railway across the old shared bridge spanning the Afon Dwyryd river, I joined the A496 tracking the railway (pardon the pun) until it met the B4573, a country road which took me uphill before descending and rejoining the A496 at Harlech Castle. For roughly the next half mile, I was really close to the coast overlooking Tremadog Bay until I started travelling further inland, still following the railway. After about four miles I rejoined the coast closing in on Barmouth.

Barmouth lifeboat station has boasted an all-weather lifeboat for nearly 180 years and now has a Mersey class and an inshore D class lifeboat. Over the years here they have received 13 awards for gallantry. I arrived to the usual friendly welcome we find when meeting volunteer crew members and other folk enthusiastic about our project. In the meantime, Brenda and Brian had gone to find the Criccieth lifeboat station. There they managed to collect £3 for the RNLI. Unfortunately, not having the national media behind us, people were unaware of what we were trying to do and so throughout the whole journey we found it difficult to raise funds for the RNLI. This did not in any way dampen our enthusiasm, especially mine. After their excursion, Brenda and Brian returned to the site. Brenda brought the diary up to date and Brian did the utilities. That was followed by lunch.

I left Barmouth mid afternoon and doubled back on my journey but would have preferred to follow the Afon Mawddach River. The view back down to the estuary where the railway crosses the river must have been the view my son Tony had mentioned. However this diversion would have added more time to my return journey. Anyway it had been another delightful journey on the scooter. I managed to take a photo or two on my return overlooking the large stretch of sandy beach where the road comes close to the coast overlooking Tremadog Bay. What a beautiful view. I arrived back on site by 5:30 PM. As I mentioned previously there were road works a mile or two from out site. They were in full operation but when I arrived at the head of the traffic with the light at red the workmen switched the traffic lights to red in both directions to allow me to travel safely through the road works without other traffic bothering me. How good was that? Just one person's understanding can make you feel so good. After a cooked dinner we managed to get the TV working with help from a fellow caravaner after Brian and I had struggled to get the aerial into the right position. Brenda's was of course delighted to be able to watch TV.

# Day 34, May 5

It was raining on and off. Was our luck changing? After breakfast we left the site for the three mile journey to Criccieth where we met two female volunteers; one we found out later was the coxswain's wife, who suggested that if we return later we would be able to watch a rescue demonstration. With three more lifeboat stations to visit that day, off I went with Brenda and Brian following on. The temperature was now 16°. We arrived at Pwyhelli lifeboat station and had coffee and our sandwiches. After lunch it was still raining. I left to go on to Abersoch lifeboat station and Brenda and Brian went on ahead to Porthdinllaen lifeboat station. It was necessary to pass through the Nefyn and District Golf Club course to reach this station, although the crew room was in the car park at the top of a hill where the club house was situated.

My journey from Criccieth followed the coast along the A497 once again overlooking Tremadog Bay and the railway line. Arriving at Pwllheli, I joined the A499 which took me down to Abersoch, doubling back to the A497 across Llŷn Peninsula (in Welsh Pen Llyn) and eventually arrived at the car park where Brenda and Brian were waiting. This was after stopping on the roadside to take a photo of a man on his tractor ploughing a field with gulls following behind feeding on whatever may have been uncovered. Unfortunately I did not have the camera set up correctly for the movement in the shot and was disappointed with the outcome. Once again I had not given myself enough time to sit and work out the right settings for this type of shot. Additionally it was still raining slightly, but I can't use this as an excuse. Brenda explained how the journey through the golf course had been scary with the undulating rough track, and the fact that they were driving through a golf course. They advised me not to go to the Porthdinllaen lifeboat station because of this and anyway there was no one on site. We loaded the scooter and returned to Criccieth lifeboat station where we watched an exercise carried out by the crew. We were invited in afterwards for coffee and the inevitable chat. At the same time new recruits were involved in a lecture and we felt privileged to be there at that time.

## Day 35, May 6

On another warm, sunny day we left site to arriving at the next site Tal-y-Bont, in the Vale of Conway, at around lunchtime. It was a nice quiet site where, on my speaking to the owner about our project, we were charged for only two of the three nights. I towed the caravan onto our pitch, which was made very simple as it was a very flat site. Brenda and I sorted out the utilities as Brian was on a mission to retrieve an umbrella which he had left it at the last lifeboat station. He had insisted on returning to collect it. I offered him a similar umbrella but to no avail so, to my annoyance, he drove on scoot4life petrol to retrieve it. Luckily for us, we didn't really need him to set up on this site. After his return we made sandwiches and sat outside in the warm sunshine and had our lunch on a picnic bench next to the caravan.

Then we went to Conwy for some shopping. Leaving there we drove to the river estuary by Penrhyn Castle for a pint and fish and chips. Whilst we sat there with our drinks there was an almighty downpour, which forced everyone into the pub until the rain and thunder ceased. When it was over, Brian went off to find some fish and chips. It wasn't long before he returned and we found a convenient spot to eat them. We returned to the caravan with the TV working and Brenda managing to Skype Tony, before we all turned in for bed.

## Day 36, May 7

Really warm and sunny, but it started to rain late morning. Tony phoned to say the local Blackpool paper was very interested in our journey and wanted to interview me when we arrived in their area; of course we agreed to meet them later. Brenda and Brian left for Conwy lifeboat station, and I left for Llandudno lifeboat station with it raining quite hard.

I eventually found the station which was nowhere near the beach but luckily a local pointed me in the right direction. To my disappointment I arrived there to find nobody on site, not because there was no one to greet me, but because I was busting for a wee. Although I carried a bottle with me for such emergencies, I never actually use it. I left Llandudno to go on to Rhyl lifeboat station but, having taken a wrong turn, I found myself heading back via a different route to roughly where I started. The realisation that I had wasted so much time was very frustrating. My only excuse was the rain and trying to read the map whilst keeping it dry. When everything is so wet it tends to dampen one's enthusiasm too and so I contacted Brenda and Brian who found me where I was and we abandoned the RNLI for the rest of the day.

On returning to base, we did odd jobs needed around the caravan, etc. After dinner, we caught up with the diary and the day ended in sunshine and showers, but for me, the day ended in disappointment, because I had failed to achieve the day's targets.

## Day 37, May 8

Breakfast over and all the chores done, Brenda and Brian left for Rhyl lifeboat station. I left on the scooter travelling north on the B5106 then turning right to onto the A470. At Tal-y-cafn I headed north again after crossing the Conwy with views over the river where it widens on its way to the estuary. Again turning right, I headed east to avoid the A55 dual carriageway and at Abergele I joined the A548 which lead me along the coast to my first lifeboat station of the day at Rhyl. This time I managed to arrive there successfully and in sunny weather, After I had arrived, Brenda and Brian, continued on to Flint lifeboat station, the next on the list. I continued to follow the coast towards Flint, arriving some two hours later, I had negotiated my way round several dual carriageways, avoiding them wherever I could but had had to travel a short distance on others.

Towards the end of the ride I came across three young lads by the side of the road and enquired about the run into Flint. They kindly sent me in the right direction, and they put a few pounds into the collection box, which was fixed to the front of the scooter. I mounted the pavement with a jerk because there was no drop curb but was then able to continue on the pavement, following the dual-carriageway into Flint. While waiting for me, Brenda walked Sam and Brian checked out Flint Castle. As luck would have it the crew had just returned to the lifeboat station from a shout which

Me arriving at Flint.

gave us the opportunity to tell them about our project. In the picture I can be seen with the crew.

We spent some time chatting before returning to the caravan for dinner and to attempt to update our emails. After Brenda had completed them she tried to send them but for some reason they had disappeared! She could not find them in Sent messages or drafts and so gave them up as lost annoyingly and had to do them all over again.

## Day 38, May 9

With breakfast out of the way, Brenda and I made use of the shower in the caravan, even though it creates extra work for Brian, who has to fill the tank with clean water and then empty the waste after our showers. Then, morning chores completed, Brenda and Brian went off to find somewhere to do the washing. They soon returned needing 12 × 20p pieces before they could start the washing machine which would take three hours! I was left in the caravan trying to book the next caravan sites, but with no signal on the mobiles and with no Internet connection, not for the first time, it was proving to be a headache.

After lunch we drove to Bodnant Gardens run by the National Trust, where I sat with Sam in the car waiting until Brenda and Brian returned. They spent about an hour in the lovely garden and took lots of photos. We hope to visit these gardens again in the future and particularly at this time of year when it is full of all sorts of wonderful spring blooms. I highly recommend a visit if you are in the area. After leaving the gardens, we carried on exploring a narrow track leading up into the mountains until eventually it came to a dead end. We still managed to take the odd photo here and there and then, after our adventure through the mountains, we decided to visit a pub for our evening meal so that we could relax fully, remembering our frustrating morning.

## Day 39, May 10

This morning we awoke to rain. For some reason we had a Wi-Fi signal and so I spent time booking the next site. Late morning we ventured off to Swallow Falls, cameras in hand. These famous waterfalls are well worth a visit particularly when there has been a lot of rain to swell the River Afon Llugwy and the water cascades down through the rocks on its journey to the sea.

We had arranged to meet Brenda's sister, Hazel, and her husband, Norman, for a meal in a local pub that evening, as they were both on holiday in the area, so leaving Swallow Falls we headed for Betws-y-Coed. We met up and all took a short walk around the area, visiting the Conwy Valley Railway Museum and the row of shops and cafes in front. Then we headed off to a nearby hotel and settled down for our evening meal as planned. Meal over, we said our goodbyes to Hazel and Norman and returned to the caravan, where Brenda received a text message from Hazel saying that the landlord at the B&B where they were staying would be writing a cheque for scoot4life. It was another kind gesture from a complete stranger

# CHAPTER NINE

# North West

## Day 40, May 11

Having packed up, we left later in the morning travelling 62 miles onto the Wirral, arriving on site at Church Farm. The caravan was positioned next to pens where small animals were kept for children to visit. With the caravan settled, it was time for lunch and afterwards, with no pressure on trying to visit lifeboat stations today, we decided to drive out to New Brighton in order to check out stations on the way, so that I could get a good idea of the route for the scooter before setting out on the official scoot tomorrow. It was extremely windy when we arrived at New Brighton but this didn't put us off. We stood on the north-east corner of the Wirral at Fort Perch Rock, an early 19th century coastal fortification, overlooking the River Mersey with Liverpool city in the background. Clearly visible was the well known Liver building and ships passing by, in and out of the once busy docks, trading goods and people.

As we drove back to the caravan site, the car started making strange worrying noises and lights appeared on the dashboard suggesting there might be a problem but after a while it all seemed to settle down and everything went back to normal. We hoped that it would stay that way!

## Day 41, May 12

After clearing up the caravan and preparing the scooter for another day on the road, I left site to visit the three lifeboat stations on the Wirral. The first was West Kirby where I was lucky to meet two volunteers back from a demonstration. They had been showing children the small inshore lifeboat which they had with them. After this brief encounter, I moved on to Hoylake where I met with Brenda and Brian and two crew members on station. We spent time talking with them and having the usual coffee, while they explained all about this brand-new eco-friendly lifeboat station which had been in operation since February 2009. The station was taken over by the RNLI in 1894 and has to its credit two silver medals and five bronze medals.

The third lifeboat station on the Wirral is at New Brighton but there was nobody on site. I did know, however, that they had a hovercraft at this station, which is especially needed at that end of the Wirral where the water is very shallow.

We returned to the caravan site and the small animals. Brenda took Sam for a long walk before making our evening meal. I settled down once again with my map in front of me planning the next day's move. I felt slightly apprehensive about towing the caravan

**Us at Hoylake.**

through the Mersey Tunnel but with hindsight I needn't have worried.

## Day 42, May 13

With breakfast over and having done all the normal chores involved in breaking camp, we were on the road again, a journey of some 63 miles to a well-established site at Kneps Farm Holiday Park, near Blackpool, close to the river Wyre. The slight apprehension I had the previous day was now gone, since the journey through the tunnel had been very straightforward. On our arrival at the new site we were directed to where we were to position our caravan. This was a flat hard-standing spacious area. The site was well-organized. It had electrically operated gates which automatically opened on exit, but on entry were operated through a key system. Once settled in we had lunch then it was time to get the washing done and dried while the weather was fine. Having all these facilities on-site is always a bonus. The weather held until around five in the evening when the rain started but it only lasted for about half an hour. Tony contacted us to tell us that he'd been in touch with the Blackpool Gazette, and a local journalist would turn up later that afternoon come early evening, to interview me and take some photos, having permission from the site owners. Sure enough he did! After this was over, we drove into Cleveleys to find a fish and chip shop for our evening meal. We returned to the caravan where Brenda was unable to contact her parents to update them on our present position and circumstances. This was something which they were very keen to know throughout our journey. They were plotting our journey on a map for themselves and also for the benefit of their friends.

## Day 43, May 14

The morning began as usual. Later on our attention was set on replying to an email we had received from people I had met during my stay at the NEC with John and his salesman. They had made me feel right at home whilst I was there. The hope was for them to meet up with us during the trip but unfortunately we were all in the wrong places at the wrong time. We had also been waiting for news from our niece, Lucy, about the baby she was expecting, but there was still no news of the baby's arrival.

We left site mid-morning and travelled to Lytham Saint Annes lifeboat station, the first of three. Brian dropped me there and set off for Blackpool lifeboat station where we hoped to meet up again later. At Lytham Saint Annes, the sand on the beach road the A584, which would take me to all the stations I was visiting that day, had been blown across the road, particularly, at the road edges. This caused me some difficulty navigating my way through this area. Having eventually overcome this problem there were still more hazards to come. Unfortunately we had not realized that Blackpool Promenade was in total chaos with new work being done to improve and update the Promenade. The lifeboat station was cut off from traffic which was totally confusing for Brian. He had done several circuits round the town trying to find a way to the station. In the end he gave up and moved on to Fleetwood, where we met again later. In the meantime I was able to find my way to the station where I met two volunteers working in the shop. After my initial introduction they told me that nobody was visiting the lifeboat station as it was very difficult to reach through all the road works and barriers approaching the station. Subsequently they were not collecting any revenue via the shop. They told me that the chaos was lasting much longer than was originally planned. Despite this, out of their own pockets, they put some money in our collection box. This is something I had not expected from the various members and volunteers of the RNLI.

After spending some time chatting with these ladies I left to travel on to Fleetwood lifeboat station without further complication. On my arrival, meeting up with Brenda and Brian, it started to rain, as well as being windy and cold. We sat in Brian's car to have lunch but, as you may have guessed, there was nobody on site. We left Fleetwood and returned to the caravan where eventually we settled down and had our evening meal. Part of the means by which we cooked our food was a George Foreman grill which we had brought with us. It helped us manage our resources because electricity was included in the price of the sites. This obviously meant we could save on gas. After our evening meal the wind and rain had eased but it was still cloudy. We decided to go for a "walk" along the river estuary, approximately three miles there and back. Brian and I used our scooters and Brenda walked Sam. I may not have mentioned before that Brian had brought along his small scooter which, when taken apart, fitted alongside mine in the back of his car. The walk finished off the day pleasantly.

## Day 44, May 15

Once again we are on the move. On finally leaving site we handed back the electronic key used to open the gates on entry. We were pleasantly surprised to receive a £20 donation from the site owners towards our fundraising for the RNLI. Our journey this day took us a further 125 miles up the coast to St Bees which is just on the edge of the Lake District. The caravan site was right on the seafront, part of a static site, and, incidentally, right next to St Bees lifeboat station. We arrived at 2:40 pm that afternoon. After settling the caravan with views across the sea we had rolls for lunch. Brenda did some washing and drying at the on-site launderette. She would walk to and fro checking on the drying process until everything was finished. One of her pet hates is sitting in a launderette waiting for the washing to be completed. I can only sympathize with her.

After cooking dinner that evening we were able to watch TV, but there was no Internet or mobile signal, or what there was was very weak. During the night it was very windy and we could hear the sea.

St Bees caravan site.

I found the noise soothing and was able to sleep without difficulty but Brenda's sleep was interrupted by the noise. I suppose I did not expect this to be a problem for her. She was born in Brighton and then lived until she was fourteen at Bognor Regis. She had spent a lot of time at the beach and I thought that if someone lived close to the sea would get used to the sound of the waves. However she did not live as close to the beach as the caravan was then situated and it was the sound of the pebbles moving with the ebb and flow of the tide that disturbed her.

## Day 45, May 16

With morning chores behind us, it was time for operation lifeboat stations. We decided not to go to Barrow-in-Furness as it was a long way from site, approximately 48 miles and it would have cost extra fuel to back-track such a distance just to visit one lifeboat station. This was one of the few stations we sadly never managed to get to. I didn't take these decisions lightly and, bearing in mind what we may not have collected for the RNLI judging by past experience, we probably made the right decision.

It was therefore decided that Workington lifeboat station would be our number one target. Brenda and Brian left site going on ahead to find the lifeboat station. I travelled to Whitehaven lifeboat station via minor roads leading from site and then continued on towards Workington lifeboat station on the A595, but unfortunately for me I came across a dual carriageway which was unmarked on my, dare I say it, out-of-date map. I was now committed and had to go ahead because I was unable to turn around. I didn't want to continue as I was unsure either of the speed limit or the length of the dual carriageway. Fortunately, I managed to pull into a layby where I had no choice but to call Brenda and Brian on my mobile asking them to return and pick me up. Once the scooter was loaded into the back of Brian's car, we went on to find Workington lifeboat station.

This wasn't quite as easy as we had hoped, but eventually we found the way across the docks and disused railway lines and between the cranes, etc, all now in the pouring rain. After negotiating the piles of sand blown by the wind at the back of this station, we found our way round to the front, where we met Richard, an RNLI mechanic, who invited us in, out of the wind and rain for coffee. We sat with him whilst we had our lunch and spent some time chatting, not all about the RNLI but also life in general. Before we left he kindly phoned ahead to Silloth lifeboat station warning them of our pending visit. We said our goodbyes to Richard and I continued on the scooter towards the next of our targets, while of course, Brenda and Brian went on ahead in the car.

From Workington, I followed the A596 and then the B5300 a journey of about 14 or 15 miles following the line of the coast overlooking the Solway Firth. It was still raining and windy but eventually I ended up riding along the esplanade to reach Silloth lifeboat station which was established in 1860. What a brilliant arrival! I was met by eight crew members who had all turned out to meet me. I was greeted with warm enthusiasm by the coxswain and crew and was soon given a hot cup of coffee with a drop of whisky in it. Before we left, they presented us with mementos, flags etc,

Later Brenda told me that the coxswain had tears in his eyes because of the challenge we had set ourselves, It is very heart-warming when you affect someone in such a way and helps drive you on. This station was the last one we would be visiting in England for the time being; our next stop would be Scotland. One of the inspirational experiences on the scooter was the spring smells, such as wild garlic, bluebells, etc, which lined the roadside on my journey through the countryside. I really enjoyed this aspect of my travels, the same thing a walker would experience, when out and about in the countryside. My wheels were my legs giving me this unique experience!

## Day 46, May 17

Raining this morning, so we decided to go into Whitehaven to catch up with our banking and shopping later returning to site for some in-house jobs. After this, Brenda went for a long walk with Sam along the beach while Brian and I strolled along at a much slower pace taking photos. In the afternoon at St Bees lifeboat station there was an exercise in progress. We took this opportunity to go along and introduce ourselves., Of course, we were invited in and made most welcome. We sat with the crew chatting and drinking their coffee as usual and, from our privileged position, had a great view of the exercise. After the exercise and the cleaning of the boat and equipment etc, some of the crew, who would usually make their way to the nearby Hotel for a drink, invited us along that evening to join them. After dinner both Brian and I ventured across to the Hotel where we met up with the crew and had a relaxing time enjoying general conversation. Unfortunately Brenda was stuck back at the caravan keeping an eye on Sam but she did manage to Skype with Tony. We returned late but not before we had been given £10 from a crew member as a donation to the RNLI.

## Day 47, May 18

Brian, who had never visited the Lake district before, was about to get a great experience! Brenda and I decided to take him to my favourite lake, Wastwater, a beautiful part of the Lake District nearby. I would recommend it to anyone visiting the lakes for the first time.   We left the caravan at around 10.30am, and although the weather was windy and a little cold, it didn't put us off.

We spent some time taking photos before finally venturing to the end of the road, and going around the back of Wastdale Head Hotel, where we found a packhorse bridge which looks so delicate but has survived for hundreds of years. The Hotel makes an excellent base for walkers visiting this area. We returned to the nearby village of Gosforth for lunch in a cafe in the centre of the village and, having satisfied our hunger, returned to Wastwater to top up on a little more photography. One thing I have become aware of is that I never seem to have enough time for photographs, but today I was able to take advantage of the time we had set aside for this purpose. Brenda walked Sam along the riverbank leading away from the hotel towards the mountains, leaving Brian and me taking ever more photos.

On our return to the caravan, I managed to contact our friend Lynda, who was planning to join us on the coming Saturday, to help tow the caravan for a week. After tea, Brenda walked up to the cliff top which is either the beginning or the end of the coast-to-coast walk, depending where you set out from, and made a video clip of the surrounding area.

# CHAPTER TEN

# Scotland

## Day 48, May 19

We left St Bees in beautiful weather, blue skies and a temperature around 15°, for a reasonably straightforward journey of some 92 miles. We arrived early afternoon at a lovely caravan site called Sandy Hills, south of Dumfries, and I drove straight onto a flat pitch, nice and easy. I also managed to negotiate a big saving on the cost of £83 for three nights, for just £30! However, after talking with the management, it seemed that we were at the wrong site; despite this they kindly let us stay! We were right next to a sandy beach facing south, once again overlooking the Solway Firth. After completing all the utilities and eating lunch, we popped up the road for some supplies. We then were able to stroll along the beach and spend about an hour and a half playing with Sam and taking photos before returning for a cooked dinner. Brenda managed to text, but we had no Internet connection; nevertheless it was the ending of a very pleasant day.

# Day 49, May 20

After earlier rain, it turned out sunny and breezy and wasn't too bad at 9:30 am, which was an early start for me. I left the site on my way to Kippford lifeboat station, using the A710 heading inland then turning left onto a minor road which brought me into Kippford. Brenda and Brian arrived at the same time. We met people in the RNLI shop who gave us a donation for the RNLI. By now the wind had got up again and so we took refuge in a bus shelter overlooking the Solway Firth where we tucked into our sandwiches. Lunch over, I headed for Kirkcudbright lifeboat station, returning to the A710, scooting further inland to Dalbeattie, then joining the A711 heading south once more to follow the road about a mile inland from the coast, before reaching Kirkcudbright Bay, and then finally Kirkcudbright town itself. Here I had to ask a man where the lifeboat station was and following his instructions got there in the end.

I arrived at what I thought was the lifeboat station as instructed and met John, a crew member. Introducing myself to him, I expected to hear a broad Scottish accent in reply but to my surprise heard a southern accent. I learnt that he came from Maidstone in Kent and was now living in Scotland. I actually had arrived not at the station but at the crew room and it's from here that the crew are driven in a Land Rover some four miles along a very bumpy winding narrow road to the station proper. I learned that one particular crew member has to sit in the front of the Land Rover as he is over six feet tall, so as to prevent him banging his head on the roof since the Landrover has to drive as quickly as possible along the bumpy road when on a shout. When Brenda and Brian arrived, John asked us if we'd like to visit the lifeboat station and of course we answered

Our transport to Kirkcudbright.

yes, so he contacted his boss to check that it would be okay. His answer being yes meant that the next trick was to get Brian and me on board the Land Rover. John produced a stool for us to climb up and into the back and off we went. Arriving at the lifeboat station, it seemed to be situated on the edge of a lake in a very isolated spot and after Brian and I climbed out the back of the Land Rover, John showed us around the station. Afterwards, we went through the same performance getting back into the Land Rover for our return journey to Kirkcudbright where we left John after thanking him for his time.

While sitting eating our lunch meal of fish and chips, I received a call from Ken Hames our patron who was trying to contact the BBC about our project, but alas they seem uninterested. I'm sure nationwide coverage by the BBC would have helped us raise more money but despite this we had had another interesting day.

## Day 50, May 21 – Lynda's Arrival

This morning we managed to get a signal and talk to Brenda's sister Hazel, also text Tony our son, who told us the temperature in his garden was around 30°. We left late morning to drive into Dumfries for some shopping but more importantly to collect Lynda, who was arriving by train to join us for a week. We arrived at the station early and so decided to drive around Dumfries as we had never visited the town before, but although we did not stop anywhere in the town, we managed to get ourselves lost and lose the station. Eventually we found our way back to the side of the station on which Lynda was arriving and, with Lynda safely on board my car, we travelled to Colvend village, close to the caravan site, where we all piled into a café out of the rain, enjoying soup and coffee before returning to site by which time it was raining really hard. After dinner and watching some TV, we moved Brian from his end of the caravan to allow Brenda and Lynda to take over, while Brian and I slept in the living area at right angles to one another on the seats. This became our sleeping arrangements during Lynda's stay with us.

## Day 51, May 22

While connecting the electrics from the caravan to the car, we found we had a problem with the socket affecting the lights on the caravan. Thankfully a man on the site helped us to fix this problem before we moved off on our 63-mile journey to Aird Donald

Caravan Site, Stranraer, along roads which were pretty empty of traffic throughout the journey. After quickly sorting out the normal utilities, we made sandwiches for lunch and by early afternoon I left the site to go to Stranraer lifeboat station. Athough it was sunny, it was quite chilly too. Brenda, Brian and Lynda met me there but without any crew members on site we continued on to Portpatrick.

Leaving the others I scooted along the main A77 through some fine countryside and at a place called Lochans I turned right, still on the A77, passing many farms as I eventually descended into Portpatrick; however, first I stopped at the public conveniences, with that feeling of desperation which must be partly age related, combined with blood pressure pills – the joys of ageing! We all met up again at the station but there was nobody to be found there as well. We had a good look around this very attractive harbour and Brenda was able to walk Sam. We returned to the caravan for dinner but while cooking ran out of gas. Fortunately for us help was at hand. The site owners stocked the gas and kindly fitted a new bottle so we could continue with our dinner. The weather was deteriorating becoming increasingly very wet and windy and the man from the site advised us while fitting the gas bottle about the weather warnings and a hurricane which was approaching the area. He suggested that we stay another night here and the danger became very obvious by the movement of the caravan overnight as the wind strengthened its grip over the land.

## Day 52, May 23

We were up late this morning after an unsettled night with the wind buffeting the caravan and with heavy winds and rain still. When we had first arrived there had been a few other caravans on this large site but before we left we were on our own. Because of the heavy winds we decided not to move, heeding the advice of the man from the site. We had only intended to stay just one night but the weather had changed all that! Brenda and Lynda went to the shower block to freshen up for the day and then we drove to Stranraer to find a pub but couldn't find one with a convenient car park and so the decision was made to drive back to Portpatrick,

Here we managed to park outside a pub opposite the sea which was very rough and waves were crashing over the road. We all got out of the car and Brenda and Lynda went ahead of us into the pub whilst Brian and I struggled to reach the door because of the gale force winds which were still raging. The girls looked out of the pub window to see where we had got to, only to crack up laughing at our attempts to stagger to the pub door in such conditions. We saw the funny side of it as well and they had to come back out into the storm to rescue us from our feeble attempts to get into the pub on our own. Brenda commented that she'd never known me to take so long to get into a pub! Lynda treated us to lunch before we returned to the car and drove a few yards from the pub to the edge of the harbour, where we clambered out of the car to take photos of the stormy seas in front of us.

Unbeknown to me at the time, the electronic device on my keys for opening the car doors had became contaminated by the seawater, which I discovered later during the trip. After reparking the car further round the harbour to take more photos we returned to site for tea and settled down for the evening We hoped all would be well for moving the next day but what an unforgettable day it had been!

Rough sea at Portpatrick.

After the whole project was over and we met up with Lynda again, I asked her what her most memorable moments of the trip had been and yes, you guessed it, it was of course the events outside the pub at Portpatrick!

## Day 53, May 24

A warmer feel today, but still windy. Lynda was towing the caravan the 47 miles to our next site, Culzean Castle Camping and Caravanning Club Site, Maybole, Ayrshire, this being a very efficiently laid out walled site. We managed to negotiate a good discount and, after setting up the caravan for our stay, we made our lunch. Then I left on the scooter to go to Girvan lifeboat station. I travelled along the A719 then joined the A77 at Turnberry with views of the coast on my right. While I was scooting south to Girvan, 'my crew' followed on picking me up at the lifeboat station but there was no crew encounter here. Returning to Culzean Castle site, Brenda took advantage of the washing facilities, but we had no mobile signals or Internet, making it impossible to book our next site. The solution was to drive off site to see if I could pick up a signal for my mobile. I probably drove 2 to 3 miles before I could obtain a signal but frustratingly nobody picked up the phone. I returned to site and got my head down in the map in the hope of finding a site for the next day.

## Day 54, May 25

We didn't leave the site until midday. Lynda towed the caravan again with Brenda at her side; it was still very windy but with a little sunshine. I went ahead with Brian to see if we could find and book a site, something we had not had to do before, having always managed to pre-book. Meanwhile the girls had pulled into a lay-by and sat waiting for a call from us. We managed to find a site at Saltcoats in Ayrshire called Sandylands, this being a static site with provision for touring caravans and entertainment in the evenings! After booking the site I phoned the girls with directions and Brian and I waited nearby to guide them to the new site. By now it was raining quite hard. Lynda manoeuvred the caravan between two very large rocks to get to our caravan pitch but unfortunately she came a little too close on the left-hand side, where an enormous rock was situated. This now meant reversing the caravan in order to try to sweep further round between the two rocks. While this was happening we had managed to block a delivery lorry from leaving the site and the driver was getting a little impatient. I was out of the car telling Lynda which way to turn the steering wheel in order to complete the necessary manoeuvre and, in my haste, I slipped and fell rather badly onto my right side. I was soon back on my feet but under pressure to move the caravan as quickly as possible, finally completing the task and allowing the lorry to leave. We eventually managed to manoeuvre the caravan successfully on the required spot but we were all soaking wet. We eventually recovered from this ordeal although I was still in a lot of pain. We had lunch and afterwards managed to get on the Internet this time to send the two latest updates. Leaving the site, we drove around for a while before finding a Chinese takeaway, returning to the caravan with a hot meal to round off the day. Because of the rain and my fall, we decided to book an extra day on this site.

## Day 55, May 26

Our first target today was Troon lifeboat station which had been in operation for nearly 135 years. From the site my first problem to overcome was dual carriageways.

On a scooter one has limited access due to speed restrictions, or so I thought.

Class 3 scooters, which can travel up to 8 mph, have to be fitted with front and rear lights, indicators and a horn before they are permitted on the road, as long as they are road taxed, restrictions being motorways, bus or cycle lanes. This information can be found on the Internet.

I therefore made the decision to visit Troon by car to avoid these difficulties. On arrival we were met by a lovely lady called Carolyn and her colleague Walter. They invited us into the station and after we had explained about the project, we were soon sitting chatting with a cup of coffee in our hands. They offered to take us onto the lifeboat, a type Severn, which were, at the time of our trip, the biggest boats in the RNLI fleet with a length of 17 metres, a maximum speed of 25 knots, and a range of 250 nautical miles carrying a crew of six. Donning life jackets we went on board and were given an in-depth look around the boat. Carolyn, who incidentally is a marine biologist, took us through to the engine room where her job is to look after the engines. She explained how she would position herself while the boat was at sea, also attending

Lynda on board at Troon.

to any job that may occur during a shout. After spending about an hour on board looking at every aspect of the boat, we returned to the station to have a good look round their inshore boat. We all had a great time at Troon, ending up with a few souvenirs such as pencils, flags and things to hand out on our trip. This had been one of those special days for us.

We returned to the caravan site, and this time I left on the scooter, for my second target of that day, Largs lifeboat station. This involved a journey of roughly ten miles further up the A78, following the coast closely at first, passing by West Kilbride and then travelling slightly inland before hugging the coast again, overlooking a small island called Great Cumbrae. This is the home of the National Water Sports Centre and the University Marine Biological Station, Millport. Unfortunately there were no crew members around when I arrived and so later I was picked up by Brian and we returned to the caravan for dinner. That evening Brenda and Lynda went to the clubhouse for a drink, while Brian and I took care of Sam. It was the end of a good day for us all.

## Day 56, May 27

Before leaving site and while we had a signal, Brenda sent a few text messages and a couple of tweets. We left with Lynda again towing the caravan, this time for 59 miles to our next site on the edge of Loch Long, Forest Holiday Site, Ardgartan. What a beautiful place we found ourselves in and with the Trossachs National Park on our doorstep, we decided to stay for the next four days. Because of the bank holiday weekend, I had tried to arrange a site on the edge of Loch Lomond, with two possibilities, but the first one had been closed due to the storm we had experienced a few days ago and the second had been full for the same reason. On our arrival at Loch Long, it became apparent when booking in that this site had suffered similar problems due to that terrible storm. Luckily they had their electricity back and had made some repairs to their main building, telling us that the wind had been running up the valley at around 120 mph at the storm's peak, destroying trees etc in its wake. We also heard that one person had been killed when a tree fell on their car. As we drove to our position on the site we noticed two caravans which had been damaged by the wind; one was upside down and the other on its side, but luckily no one had been occupying them at the time.

After settling in on site in the rain and doing the usual necessaries, we sent Brian and Lynda on an exploratory trip to find fish and chips for our main meal. We were delighted that their mission was successful and a lovely fish and chips dinner was thoroughly enjoyed by us all. Later Brenda's parents manage to phone and catch up with the story so far.

## Day 57, May 28th

The girls went for a shower, followed by laundry chores, and after our ablutions, Brian was in charge of a fry up for breakfast. I left the site on approximately a 12 mile journey following the A814 south to Helensburgh lifeboat station. The wind was cold and it was still wet and although the journey was scenic, it was an uncomfortable one for me. As I travelled along the side of Loch Long, on the bank opposite although somewhat off in the distance, I noticed a rather large bird with white on its wings. but I could not identify it at the time. Later I discovered it in one of our bird books and it was a hen harrier, apparently quite a rare bird. I finally arrived at the lifeboat station but unfortunately for me, there were no crew members on site. I badly needed to shelter from the cold wind but there was nowhere available where I could be shielded from the wind. It became a case of waiting for the rest of our crew, who had left the caravan site to do a big shop, before coming to find me. By the time they finally arrived, I was very cold and wet, and more than pleased to see them. On leaving the station, we made for the nearest cafe for coffee and a warm up. Lynda was driving my car on the way back and, probably on my directions, took a wrong turning, ending up at what appeared to be a dead end. At this point we met two very friendly police officers guarding a military installation close to Loch Long; as far as I know this is the place where torpedoes were tested by the Royal Navy at their super submarine base!

We eventually returned to the caravan by which time the rain had stopped for the moment and so we decided to have a wander round, to find they also had lodges with Jacuzzis attached overlooking the loch. Loch Long, Forest Holiday Site is rather a lovely holiday destination weather permitting but the rain had returned and so we retreated to the caravan to cook our main meal and once again settled down for an evening of television.

## Day 58, May 29

We woke to more rain. Brenda managed to send another tweet. Leaving the site at around midday with the weather still windy we drove to Tighnabruaich lifeboat station. Again this was a small unmanned inshore lifeboat station on the edge of the Kyles of Bute off the A8003, with great scenery all around. This is a spectacular part of Scotland with its lochs and mountains, and if you are looking for amazing scenery, you cannot go wrong with this beautiful place. We had our sandwiches in a little shelter on the edge of the water, before wandering off to find some toilets and take a few photos, driving back a different way to get another view of this magical area. With beautiful weather it's like being in Paradise with a photo opportunity almost around every corner. I love this part of the UK.

## Day 59, May 30

Because of our long stay over the bank holiday weekend we decided to drive to Campbeltown in the car. I would like to make it clear that on all such journeys we used our own money to finance the fuel and any other personal expenses. As the weather was now sunny and warm, after showers and breakfast, we managed to leave mid-morning on the long journey of 95 miles. Lynda volunteered to drive there and I would drive back. This lifeboat station was not in my original plan because of the great distance without any means of charging the batteries on the scooter because there were no caravan sites along this narrow peninsular at that time. For Lynda it was a journey back in time as Campbeltown was where she had spent her honeymoon with her first husband.

The journey was worth it just for the scenery. On leaving our site at Loch Long, we followed the A83 all the way to Campbeltown passing one of the most spectacular views in Scotland at the Rest and be Thankful Commemorative Stone. We also passed rivers and narrow sea inlets as we travelled further down, seeing the Isle of Gigha on our right. Finally arriving at Campbeltown, we parked the car and my priority was to visit the lifeboat station to see if there were any crew members around to talk to but after a quick look round I found nobody on site, so off we went to a local hotel for dinner; again this was a treat from Lynda. With our bellies full after a much enjoyed dinner, thanks to Lynda, we left the hotel and I returned to the lifeboat station to check if anyone had turned up. As I approached the station , I noticed a parked car which had an RNLI sticker on the front windscreen; the driver was sitting inside talking to another man through the side window; I asked if they were indeed RNLI volunteers and they were. After explaining about the project, the man standing outside the car, phoned the station coxswain who unfortunately was playing golf and was unable to take the call. Doubly unfortunately after golf he left to travel to Ireland, presumably to take up duties on one of their stations. I continued my conversation with the man in the car who told me that the coxswain would be very disappointed to have missed us and, had we arrived the day before, we would have had a good chance of going out to sea in the lifeboat. He could not emphasize enough just how disappointed the coxswain would have been to miss us!

Leaving him, I returned to tell the others what had happened. In the end it turned out that we never managed to go out to sea during the whole project, and, although we were a bit disappointed at Campbelltown, we were not downhearted, just enjoying the entire experience. We spent some time wandering around the harbour; Brenda and Lynda walked Sam taking photos as they went, both

Brian and I did the same, meeting up again and returning to the car for the long journey back to the caravan. On the way back we spotted a sandy beach at Tayinloan, parked the car and all piled out onto the beach. Sam once again enjoyed the warm sunshine and the soft sand beneath his paws, and for the rest of us it was an opportunity to relax and take more photos. Back in the car, we settled once again into the journey back, stopping at Inverary for tea and cake in a local cafe, where again we had a walk round and took yet more photos. Then it was back to the car for the final part of the journey to the caravan where we sat with another cup of tea talking over the events of our interesting day.

## Day 60, May 31

I was up first as usual, and in order to get out of bed without help, I need to swing my legs over the edge of the bed, but this morning when I did this, I heard a crack, and felt a sharp pain in the area of my ribs; this was probably the result of having fallen over a few days earlier. By late morning we were ready to leave with Lynda towing the caravan. The temperature was only 9° and it was raining again as we headed to the next site, a camping and caravan site near Oban.

It was flat which meant easy parking on a hard stand and when we had finished dealing with the usual utilities, we decided to go to Oban Hospital A & E, just to make sure I was okay. As expected there was no real damage but they advised me to take things easy and to take painkillers when needed. We returned to site for dinner; yet another site without the Internet or mobile signal, and so we watched TV, ending a non-eventful day.

## Day 61, June 1

It rained on and off all night and into the morning. With all ablutions and breakfast completed, I spent time sorting out the next campsites while waiting for the rain to ease off. Eventually I left the site in drizzle for Oban lifeboat station, just a short journey. Brenda and Lynda went shopping whilst Brian tried to collect money for the RNLI and then we all met up at the station, where again nobody was on site but apparently the crew were out on a shout, It was still raining so there was nothing for it but to return to the caravan. On the edge of this site there happened to be a wooded area with a stream running gently through it and, although it was still raining lightly, we took a stroll with Sam, just to have a look around and fill in the afternoon.

## Day 62, June 2

After breakfast and attaching the caravan to the car, we left the site with Lynda towing and me by her side feeling a little better. Just as we were leaving a fellow caravanner gave us £20 for the RNLI. Brenda and Brian left the site to go to a caravan shop just up the road, in the hope of replacing one of the caravan plugs which was now beginning to fall apart. It was only being kept together by tape having been repaired only a few days back. Today's journey was just 36 miles to an extremely well-kept site, Lochy Caravan and Camping Park, near the foot of Glen Nevis at Fort William. Lynda successfully backed the caravan onto its chosen position. Securing the caravan and all the utilities, we went to an onsite cafe, taking the laptop with us to catch up with emails. In the back of my mind, and I'm sure the others felt it too, was a kind of empty feeling since we were going to lose a strong member of our team. That evening, we drove Lynda to Fort William railway station to catch the overnight sleeper home. It was a sad moment for the rest of us as we had really enjoyed her company over one week which had then stretched into two. She had been a great help to the project throughout her stay. After seeing Lynda off, we drove along the road behind the site and up the mountain. It was a lovely sunny evening to capture images of the surrounding beautiful scenery we found ourselves in. We eventually arrived at the very end of the narrow road with its passing places, on the way stopping to photograph the waterfalls as we drove under the shadow of Ben Nevis. It was such a privilege to be in a beautiful place and, reflecting on our memories of Lynda's time with us, we all missed her very much and I knew Brenda would particularly miss the female company Lynda had provided.

## Day 63, June 3

It felt really warm this morning. Lynda sent a text message saying she had arrived home safely at around 9 am. We left the site for Mallaig Lifeboat Station, dropping me off on the way to travel 27 miles on the scooter. This journey was for me one of the best so far. In the warm sunshine it felt good and the scenery was outstanding. Travelling along the A830 stopping when I could to take photographs on this spectacular journey with such beautiful surroundings, I was in my glory! This is just one of the views we experienced on are journey to Mallaig.

View from Fort William to Mallaig.

On the way I was stopped by a cyclist who must have realised I was doing a charity ride seeing the RNLI flag attached to the back of the scooter He gave me just a pound but every little helps. I made my way first past Loch Eil, soaking up the marvellous scenery, then reaching one end of Loch Shiel at Glen Finnan, still enjoying every moment. I knew that this would be a long trip but what I hadn't realised was how good the surrounding countryside was going to be in this part of Scotland. It's quite hard to explain in detail what I was able to witness on this fabulous part of the journey, especially the beautiful sandy beach near Morar, which I'm sure will remain in my mind for many years to come. When I arrived at Mallaig I was met by Brenda telling me that they had stopped for lunch in a lay by and, while walking with Sam to stretch his legs, she had tripped and fallen badly, hurting her side and chest; while waiting for me she had visited the local chemist in Mallaig to buy some arnica and paracetamol etc, in order to relieve her pain. This was not quite the end of the brilliant scooter ride I was expecting! We stayed around the harbour for a while and Brian managed to collect £9 pounds in the RNLI pot. He had met a woman arriving by ferry from the Isle of Skye who told him she knew of someone connected with the RNLI and promised to mention our journey to them but I don't think there was any significance to this meeting with Brian. While sitting on a nearby bench enjoying an ice cream, we had a conversation with a passing RNLI volunteer confirming there was nobody at the lifeboat station. By now time was getting on and so we returned to the car for the return journey. Whilst being very sorry about Brenda's fall, scooting through such beautiful scenery had given me a brilliant ride.

# Day 64, June 4

Throughout the project my aim was to visit as many lifeboat stations as possible on mainland UK; however on this day we were heading for the Isle of Skye. because I found a site that would allow dogs. This turned out to be an extremely fortunate move. Breakfast over, caravan hooked up, we set off on a journey of around 86 miles in a temperature of around 18° and the sun shining. We left our site at Fort William to travel on the A82 to Invergarry and then onto the A87. Once again we were travelling through fantastic scenery but unfortunately because of towing the caravan I was unable to find a spot to pull over and take photographs. We eventually crossed the bridge connecting Skye to the mainland and arrived at our destination near a small place called Dunan. The site was a small boatyard, situated opposite the island of Scalpay, I towed the caravan as close as possible to the water's edge and then the owners manhandled it into position leaving us with fantastic views across the loch which is part of the Inner Sound. This was to be one of our best locations. I had only booked the site for two nights, at £20 per night, but it was well worth it. The site was small with a rough surface; the owners were still developing it, as we found out from them later. On our journey here, Brenda had managed to send several text messages to family and friends as well as having a long conversation with her sister. Finishing lunch we had a chat with Mrs Prentice, the site owner, explaining what our project was all about. Conversation over I left that afternoon and scooted back along the A87 to Kyle of Lockalsh lifeboat station. As I approached the

View from the caravan on the Skye site.

Skye bridge over Loch Alsh which has replaced the ferry service, I was delighted with the views on either side. I made my way to the lifeboat station, arriving late afternoon but nobody was on site again. Brenda and Brian were sitting on a bench overlooking the loch waiting calmly for me to arrive. Beyond us and up the hill was a Co-op, enabling us to pick up some shopping before returning back to site for dinner. Mrs Prentice knocked on the caravan door to tell us that she and her husband had decided to return our site fees and added another £20, a total of £60, to go into the pot for the RNLI which brought the eventual total of donations from the Isle of Skye to £76 00! In addition to their kindness, she also bought us some fresh eggs and homemade cake, and not only that, but volunteered to do our washing, for which we were very grateful!

## Day 65, June 5

A great sunny start to the day. Mrs Prentice had washed and dried two loads of washing for us but unfortunately Brenda's side, chest and shoulder were really hurting her. I later left for Portree lifeboat station again on the A87 (this is the only road from our site to Portree) travelling around Loch Ainort. On the way, as I approached the southern end of Loch Sligachan, on my left there was a wonderful waterfall cascading down the mountain. Several people had stopped to photograph this spectacular scene and I was no exception. Then I continued my journey up a fairly steep hill where I managed to stop by the side of the road to look back at the valley below me, soaking up my surroundings and looking back at Loch Sligachan on my right. Further along I stopped at an old bridge, now out of use, crossing a small stream and I tried to position myself from the road to capture the scene on my camera but with little success. After this, the countryside became less hilly with patches of open countryside and woodland before heading downhill with views of Portree on my right. I arrived in the early afternoon and met up with Brenda and Brian. We had our lunch sitting on a wall close to the lifeboat station but once again there was nobody on site; however between us we managed to collect £16, helped by the sunny weather which was bringing people out and about and around the station. After spending some time in Portree, despite not having met any crew members, we returned to the caravan. The day had still been a pleasant one and Brenda was feeling a little better.

# Day 66, June 6

We left this morning for a journey of 100 miles with the temperature around 11° and the weather cloudy. The reasons for such long distances in Scotland is fairly obvious because there a fewer lifeboat stations around the Scottish coast and a much lower population density. We were on our way to a site near Ullapool next to the beach at Ardmair Point. Stopping for lunch in a lay-by and then entering the caravan, we discovered some plates and glasses, smashed on the floor probably because of the many potholes in the roads. Arriving on site the caravan was secured and then we ventured onto the beach in front of us looking across the bay, where we spotted ring plovers and oystercatchers looking for morsels amongst the pebbles. From our position we could see across to a small island, called Isle Martin, and further in the distance a range of hills reaching into the sea, with shipping passing in the distance down Loch Broom towards Ullapool. After our observations, we returned to the caravan for dinner and following this we went on the hunt for fuel for the cars, paying £1.51 per litre for diesel the most so far. It was slightly cheaper for Brian's car as it runs on petrol. Back on site we managed to sort out the TV and the Internet.

## Day 67, June 7

Raining and windy all night. Sam was restless and in and out of his bed throughout the night. When we left the site for today's target at Lochinver, people from two separate caravans donated a total of £15 to the RNLI pot. Brenda and Brian dropped me off at a convenient place leaving me with some 19 miles to travel on the scooter. The weather was still cold, raining and windy. I headed north again, this time on the A835. Riding uphill and then looking back, there were great views down towards Ullapool, despite the bleak outlook and low cloud. It was not raining so heavily now as I continued to follow the road up to the junction at Ledmore and then turned left onto the A837. Further along the road I passed a herd of deer lying lazily in a nearby field but no decent photo available, so I continued on until I arrived at Loch Assynt with a view of the ruins of Adrvrech Castle. Stopping here to take in the view and a photo, the road closely follows the edge of the loch and at the loch's end the road accompanies the stream heading in the same direction as me towards Lochinver.

Brenda and Brian had arrived ahead of me but when Brian went to introduce himself to two crew members on station, they didn't seem interested in what we were trying to achieve. When I arrived at around 2.45pm I met Brian and Brenda who told me about

Brian's encounter and I decided to go and talk to them myself. They were sitting in the crew room and so I introduced myself but disappointingly I came out with the same opinion as Brian. This was the first negative response we had received during the trip and, I'm glad to say, we never encountered such negativity again!

Sitting in the car with our sandwiches I suggested that we travel back via a single track road giving ourselves a different view, and what a view it turned out to be! The sun was peeping through the dark clouds lighting up areas of this beautiful scenery, a photographer's dream allowing us to capture a few images in this fantastic light. It was one of the best days for photography this trip, thanks to the perfect weather conditions. Pictures (19/20) was taken soon after leaving Lochinver as we set off back to the caravan on this magical mystery back road. What a wonderful canvas nature had laid out before us!

Back road view from Lochinver.

View on the back road south of Lochinver.

## Day 68, June 8

We had been advised not to take the north coast route towing a caravan as most of the road is single track. I had really wanted to do it, just to say that we had actually travelled round the entire UK coastline but I had to be realistic and not put the project in jeopardy; any problems at this stage could ruin the project. When I had been on holiday with my sister during the time she had lived in Scotland, I had been along the north coast and knew about the single track roads and also how beautiful this part of Scotland is.

With my decision made, we set off to cut across Scotland instead of going north. Leaving Ullapool on the A835 turning right at the t-junction with the A837 which was also a single track road for about six miles before reverting to a normal road for about four miles after which it turned left onto the A839, yet another single track road to Lairg. In the event it did not prove to be much of a problem as there were many passing places on the way. Eventually we reached the A9, travelled north past Wick and onto the A99 to a site at John o'Groats. Having crossed Scotland via this route I wondered whether I should have stuck to my original plan. The journey had been approximately 127 miles, and we only stopped on the way for lunch. When we arrived at John o'Groats later that afternoon after an uneventful journey and under clear blue skies, the site was a nice easy one for positioning the caravan. And so with all jobs completed, we sat outside in the sunshine relaxing with a cup of tea. In front of us was a clear view over to the Orkney Islands which seemed to be beckoning us to cross this short span of water – well maybe one day! On a previous visit with my sister who had lived in Scotland not far from Castletown for two years, she had introduced us to Dunnet head. Brenda and I decided to take Brian along to Dunnet Head, where on previous visits we had seen Puffins nesting on the sheer cliff face there. Also wild orchids and other wildflowers can be seen here at the most northerly point of mainland UK.

On our return from Dunnet head with kinder weather than we had been experiencing lately, we stopped at Castletown for our evening meal of sausages and chips; it seems they had run out of fish! Returning to the site we strolled down to the harbour just a stone's throw away and even though it was 10 o'clock in the evening, it was still sunny and so, of course, out came the cameras. As the sun went down we were blessed with a beautiful sunset. It was a fine end to the day!

Sun set at John o'Groats.

# Day 69, June 9

By 11.30 am we were on the road ready to tackle two lifeboat stations. Finding no crew about at Scrabster lifeboat station, out came the scooter for my journey along the A9 and then onto the A882 to Wick. I estimated it would be a journey of approximately ten miles and I left just after midday. Brenda and Brian followed on later catching me up en route when we stopped for lunch in a lay-by. The weather had changed and as it started to rain, so on went my waterproofs. Brenda and Brian went ahead to Wick lifeboat station and I continued my journey, but soon had to stop to find a convenient hole in the hedgerow for a wee. This was a problem which plagued me constantly throughout the trip. The scenery on my journey was mainly hedgerows with the odd cottage here and there before I reached Wick lifeboat station where I was invited in. Brenda and Brian had already explained our reasons for being there to the two crew members and once again we were able to enjoy coffee and the usual chat. There has been a life boat station here for over 150 years and the station has a Trent class lifeboat. They have received 11 awards for gallantry. From the view up in the station, overlooking the harbour, an occasional seal can be seen and the crew told us that we might see more seals in Gills Bay which lies between Ness of Duncansby and

overlooking the island of Stroma. Before returning to the caravan we went to take a look and were lucky to spot several common grey seals from the tiny little harbour. After this we returned to base for our evening meal. Brenda and I showered in the caravan. Brian is unable to use the caravan shower, for without his caliper he is unable to stand. £9 for the RNLI pot to day.

# Day 70, June 10

Leaving the site in sunshine with the temperature around 14° for another long trip of some 107 miles east across the Highlands and then down the A9, we stopped for lunch on the bridge which spans the estuary of the Dornoch Firth. We left the caravan attached to the car and climbed in to make our lunch. We sat eating our sandwiches overlooking the estuary as the traffic passed by, shaking the caravan as it did so. I'm not quite sure how Sam felt about it! Then we continued our journey to the next site, a camping and caravan club site at Dingwall, where we were helped to place the caravan in its selected position. As usual this site was up to camping and caravan standards and was therefore well organised; although these sites are generally more expensive, it is sometimes a good idea to use them as their facilities are convenient for washing etc. We enjoyed a couple of hours sitting by the caravan in the sun while Brenda used the facilities for all our bedding and managed to get everything dry, using the excellent tumble dryers. Brian and I went off to get our evening meal. Later we drove along the B9163 overlooking the Cromarty Firth to spend a pleasant evening before returning back to base and to use the Internet.

# Day 71, June 11

We all left the site in warm sunshine for today's starting point, Invergordon lifeboat station. There has been a lifeboat station in the Moray Firth area since 1878 and the station we were going to visit was opened in 1974 and operates an all-weather Trent class lifeboat. As we arrived we couldn't help noticing behind the station some distance away a very large cruise liner at anchor which made quite an impressive sight. The station was in full swing as it was an open day and we were soon welcomed in, this time to help with their fundraising by buying a cup of coffee and some odd bits and pieces.

Soon it was time for me to set off on my journey to Kessock lifeboat station, travelling back down the A9 again, looking out for common seals where the road came close to the Cromarty Firth.

I did see one or two before I eventually reached the junction with the A862 after which I crossed over the Cromatry Firth still on the A9. Here there is a long stretch of road gently rising over a piece of land called The Black Isle eventually reaching the junction with the A832 where I turned right onto the A832 and travelled a short distance, probably a mile, before turning right again and joining a narrow back road. I now followed this along the edge of Beauly Firth, a scenic route where I passed several walkers. In this way I avoided the dual carriageway of the A9, also making the journey far more interesting. I arrived at the unattended Kessock lifeboat station which is situated right underneath the huge road bridge of the A9 crossing to Inverness.

In the meantime Brenda and Brian had been shopping; they had taken the direct route to the station and were waiting there for me. I was feeling very cold after my journey but luckily for me, a nearby cafe was open, and so in we went for a hot cup of coffee, before returning to the caravan for dinner.

# Day 72, June 12

Today we took a short break from the project, leaving the site on a beautiful sunny morning to drive a circular route around Loch Ness. Brenda and I had been there some 40 years previously. Back then we had hired an old ambulance converted rather primitively into a mobile home; it had only two single bunk beds to share between the four of us and so my brother-in-law and I had to sleep on the floor. Anyway, back to the story. On the way round this beautiful Loch our cameras were in action. First we travelled down the A82 alongside the loch stopping off briefly at Urquhart Castle and then continued our journey until we met the A887 where we made a slight detour through Glenmoriston, before turning left at the junction with the A87 and following it until we reached the A82 again. Unfortunately this detour was not quite as interesting as we had hoped. Arriving back at the point of our original plan, we returned to Loch Ness, now joining the B862, a minor road no longer at the water's edge, and travelled slowly back towards Inverness, enjoying the views of the countryside. At one point along this narrow road, we arrived at a bridge over a stream. This bridge had obviously replaced a much older and narrower stone bridge just a few feet away and its beauty caught our attention. Stopping to take a closer look, as we got out of the car we noticed a deer in the road up ahead of us but by the time we had got our cameras ready it had disappeared into the surrounding countryside. We did manage to photograph the old attractive stone bridge and stream that flowed beneath us before we continued on our mystery journey, stopping again at another point to photograph red squirrels which were attracted by peanuts placed in a container at the edge of the road near where we stopped to use the public convenience.

We returned to the caravan for dinner and later that evening had a long walk, or should I say in Brian's and my case, a long scoot on the tow path following a stream near our Dingwall campsite, allowing Sam to stretch his legs.

## Day 73, June 13

During the night we experienced heavy rain which continued into the morning. I had arranged for my car to be serviced through Motability in Inverness and so left the site very early for us at 9-15am with Brian following on behind me. We returned in Brian's car and went on to Dingwall hospital, as Brenda was experiencing a lot of pain due to her fall a few days before. Here she had two x-rays taken and fortunately found that there were no fractures to her sternum, although she was advised that it may take up to eight weeks for her problem to heal. Now the tables were turned! She usually looks after me and does the things that I cannot manage, but now I was doing the same for her as her pain continued. Returning to Dingwall we had a cheap meal at Tesco's we left looking for somewhere to have a haircut because it had been some time since our last haircuts and, despite Brenda's discomfort, we found a barbers and a hairdressers. I led the way and while sitting in the chair chatting to the lady who owned the shop, I told her about our expedition and she kindly refused payment for her services and asked me to put the money into the RNLI pot, which of course I did. The other two who went to different hairdressers did not have the same luck as myself. After shopping in Dingwall High Street we returned to Inverness to pick up my car following its service. Thankfully all was well and we returned to the caravan for tea and post some updates via the computer.

# Day 74, June 14

It was quite a warm start to the day at 17° when we moved to a new site 87 miles away, taking the A9 into Inverness, then turning onto the A96 towards Fraserburgh and then the A98, finally arriving at our new site, Wester Bonnyton Farm near Macduff. We secured the caravan and after lunch Brian drove us to Macduff lifeboat station but there was no one there. Launching the scooter I started my journey travelling back along the coast roughly 16 miles to Buckie lifeboat station. First I scooted along the A98 until the junction to Portknockie where I picked up the A942 which took me to Buckie, a road with views out to sea at times. Just a short distance from the road is the ancient Findlater Castle whose history dates back at least to 1260. Findlater Castle is on a tiny peninsular which sticks out into the North Sea and there is a sheer drop of more than 50 feet to the rocks and sea below. The name is Norse, 'fyn' being white and 'leitr' cliff, so-called because quartz can be found in the rocks here. There was nobody at this station either but at least we could cross two more stations off our list and the weather had remained kind to us.

Back at the caravan, I spent most of the evening arranging the next site, trying to find one which would allow us to go back along the coast one day and forward the next, depending where the lifeboat stations happen to be.

# Day 75, June 15

This was to prove an interesting day! The weather was fine again, just a little bit windy. I set off from the site late morning leaving Brenda and Brian to follow on later. We had been warned not to use this site because there were travellers here but from our point of view, it was situated right where we needed it to be. We had absolutely no trouble and in fact found them quite friendly; there were only a few on site and the men were out working during the day.

My overall journey to Fraserburgh was going to be roughly 32 miles. I had planned to travel along the B9031, and according my map I had interpreted the single symbols ">" and "<" as indicating a modest descent followed by a modest ascent, the gradients had been steeper I (wrongly) expected to see these symbols "<<" and ">>" instead. I therefore believed that the scooter would be able to manage the descent and ascent near Pennan. How wrong I was! When I arrived at the point of descent there was a sign telling me to expect a 17% descent but having come so far and not wanting to turn back, after some hesitation, I continued to the bottom of the hill. There to my horror was another sign telling me to expect a 20% ascent up the hill facing me. After yet more hesitation, I decided to give the scooter and myself our biggest test yet. Fortunately the hill was a short one and I managed to get the scooter approximately three quarters of the way to the top before the motor's cut out activated and the scooter stopped. I now had to wait either for the motor to cool down or to be rescued. While waiting several cars passed by but not one stopped to ask me if I needed any help and it was about half an hour later when Brenda and Brian arrived on the scene. With their help we managed to push the scooter to the top of the hill; by then the motor had cooled down and I was able to continue my journey, eventually arriving at Fraserburgh lifeboat station.

There has been a station here for nearly 200 years and they have received 16 awards for bravery. We met the coxswain and soon the coffee was flowing, while we had our lunch at the station. Before leaving, the coxswain handed us a cheque for £100 from their crew fund, to put in our pot for the RNLI. This seemed a little strange to us, but he assured us that the money was strictly from the crew's personal fund in which they save, for example, for Christmas celebrations and buying bits and pieces needed to make their lives a little more comfortable while on station. After thanking him, I scooted along the A90 to Peterhead which took me inland at first and then back to the coast. When I arrived at this fairly industrial port with Brenda and Brian, we were told that the press was going to meet us but we waited quite some time without anybody turning up, and so we made the decision to return to the caravan after what I can only describe as a very eventful day.

# Day 76, June 16

It rained pretty much all night and half the morning. We left the site to go to St Cyrus 77 miles away, just north of Montrose to Milton Haven Seaside Caravan Park. On the journey the sun came out, lifting the temperature to approximately 15°, but we were experiencing much more traffic as we neared Aberdeen, much more than we had been used to when travelling through Scotland. After arriving at our site with its beautiful gardens, settling the caravan and having lunch, Brian drove us to Aberdeen lifeboat station. I decided that with the dual carriageways and the city traffic, it was not a good idea to ride the scooter. Aberdeen lifeboat station, established in 1802, is one of the earliest established in

Scotland. It has several hundred rescues to its credit, plus gold, silver and bronze medals. Here we met Callum, the mechanic, who as usual made us very welcome with a cup of coffee and then showed us around the Severn boat moored along by the station. It's always great to meet up with friendly crew members and Calum was no exception. After leaving Callum we returned to the caravan for dinner.

## Day 77, June 17

Before I left the site for Montrose, and leaving Brenda putting out the washing on the line, we found the lady owner of the site to pay the fees but she refused to take anything so £30 more went into the RNLI pot. Brenda and Brian left to go to the bank in Montrose before joining me at the lifeboat station, which was approximately five or six miles down the A92. Montrose is a busy port and care was needed driving through it to reach the lifeboat station. There has been a station here since 1800, making it one of the oldest in the UK. Ruth Grant Smith, who died in December 2005 aged 99, left one and a half million pounds to the station! We had coffee and our lunch with the crew and again they put their hands in their pockets and gave us £50 for the RNLI pot. In the last few days we had managed to collect quite bit for the RNLI. Alas, not quite one and a half million! Leaving there I went on to Arbroath lifeboat station where I met up with Brenda and Brian and here we found a crew member who took some photos of us in front of their boat on the slip way. Brenda's aunt was living nearby which gave her the chance to spend a couple of hours with her. Visit over we returned to the harbour for supper before returning to the caravan later that evening.

# Day 78, June 18

Both Brian and I got very wet disconnecting the utilities and hooking up the caravan for today's move. Fortunately this experience hadn't happened too often. The journey was 57 miles, with the temperature around 11° and we stopped on the way to pick up some smokies at Aberdeen which we sent home by post, not before keeping some for our tea! Our destination was the caravan club site in Markinch in Fife. My plan was to stay here for two nights and visit three stations. It was still raining when we arrived but not quite so heavily. Brian connected the electricity, so we thought, but when switching on, nothing happened. We searched for the cause of the problem, turning the caravan upside down, looking for fuses etc, only to discover some time later that Brian had not connected our power supply correctly! It seemed that this was a different setup than usual. Brenda texted our son Terry, to wish him good luck on his bike ride from London to Brighton the following day.

# Day 79, June 19

By 10:30 am Terry had texted to say that he was halfway through his London to Brighton charity bike ride and was doing okay. We left to drive to Broughty Ferry arriving there with no one on site. Leaving there, we drove on through Dundee and crossed Firth of Tay on the Tay Road Bridge. First we followed the A914, then the A91 through St Andrews, and onto the A917 to arrive at Anstruther lifeboat station. There we met up by accident with the RNLI press officer. He asked us to wait while he went to change into his RNLI gear and get his camera so that he could take photos to put on their website and to pass on to the Fife Courier. On 18 November 2015 this lifeboat station celebrated 150 years in service and a station history book is available online at RNLI shop.org.uk. We were hoping to collect some money as the place was crowded but it soon became apparent that other charities were also collecting money, so we missed out on this opportunity. I left on the scooter to go to Kinghorn, while Brenda walked Sam around Anstruther harbour. She enjoyed this especially with the warm sunshine and it being such a lovely place, teeming with people either on holiday or on a day trip, just soaking up the atmosphere and enjoying the beautiful weather.

When I reached Kinghorn, I travelled downhill in completely the wrong direction for the harbour and lifeboat station. After turning

Me and the crew at Kinghorn.

round and starting my ascent back up the hill, I was lucky to meet two local girls, who quickly sent me in the right direction. Here I met with Brenda and Brian and the crew for coffee and a chat at the station. The crew had just returned from a shout and were waiting for me to arrive so that I could be photographed with them in front of their boat. We joined them on the station balcony which overlooks the small island of Inchkeith as well as taking some more photographs before returning to the caravan. There we text the boys and sent a video to Tony. It was another good day for us, although not too good for the RNLI pot.

# CHAPTER ELEVEN

# North East

## Day 80, June 20

Once again by late morning, having done the necessaries, we were ready to roll on today's journey of approximately 54 miles, and in fact with the temperature around 17° but under a cloudy sky. We arrived at lunchtime to a lovely site, Yellowcraig Caravan Club Site near North Berwick where we planned to stay for just one night and visit two lifeboat stations. Brenda did some washing and with the weather beginning to warm up it was geting quite hot. After lunch, I set out to scoot to North Berwick lifeboat station.

North Berwick is situated east of Edinburgh, on the north tip of East Lothian and it was just a short journey for me. Then I scooted on to Dunbar lifeboat station some eight to ten miles away. I travelled along the A198 with fine views as I passed Tantallon Castle with the Bass Rock Lighthouse in the distance. As I travelled towards the junction with the A199 the weather began to change and it started to look like rain. This turned out to be an understatement. Brenda and Brian caught up with me and pulled into a lay-by to help me on with my waterproof jacket. This seemed to attract the attention of the people living in the house on the opposite side of the road. They were no doubt wondering what all the fuss was about, as we struggled to put my waterproof jacket on but failed to get on my waterproof trousers. Brenda and Brian then went on to Dunbar lifeboat station to wait for me. In the meantime, just as I was approaching the t-junction to turn left to Dunbar, the storm broke and torrential rain fell upon me. The ride to Dunbar from this point on was the most unpleasant part of my journey around the UK. I became absolutely drenched through to my skin and wished we had succeeded in getting my waterproof trousers on. My other concern was how well would the scooter stand up to such a heavy amount of rain. In the event it performed perfectly.

There was nobody at the Dunbar lifeboat station when I arrived so, with Brenda and Brian's help, we quickly loaded the scooter and returned to site so that I could shower, change my clothes and warm up, after my dramatic day's journey.

## Day 81, June 21

The rain was still falling in the early hours and all morning too. It was one of the few occasions where we had to pack up in the rain. Our journey was 34 miles with temperatures around 13° – a marked difference from the day before. First we drove down the A1 and then onto the A1107 which took us to Eyemouth Holiday Park. This is a Park Resorts permanent holiday site with provision for touring caravans. It was reasonably priced and we planned to stay there for three nights. During the afternoon we managed to catch up with some odd jobs and I booked the next site. Brenda caught up with emails etc. In the evening we went over to the clubhouse for a drink but it was quite dead with only us and two other people in the bar.

# Day 82, June 22

It rained during the night again but it soon started to clear although the wind picked up in the morning. We drove to St Abbs which is a small fishing harbour where the lifeboat station is situated. We met Martin, a school teacher, who doubles up as press officer and volunteer, and he had received an email from Fraserburgh lifeboat station notifying him of our arrival. He invited us into the lifeboat station and showed us the emails and press cuttings about Scoot4Life which had been posted on the RNLI website. During our visit we had the usual cup of coffee. He told us that most of their call outs are to do with divers because this is a very popular area for such activities due to the many shipwrecks and the rich sea life in the coastal waters. Whilst writing this book I have learnt that St Abbs lifeboat station was closed in September 2015 against the wishes of the RNLI volunteers and it is my understanding they have all resigned from the RNLI and are now planning to use their own fishing boats to carry out future rescues in the harbour area. They intend to do this until they are able to establish their own rescue service. They feel that the journey from Eyemouth station, although only approximately two miles away, could be too long for a diver in distress in the harbour. We wish them all the best for their future.

After our visit here, I scooted back to Eyemouth to visit the lifeboat station, meeting up again with Brenda and Brian but sadly no crew, so we set off for some shopping, before returning to site. That evening, at a local pub in Eyemouth with a view of the entrance to the harbour, we had an enjoyable meal and discovered that the pub was owned by one of the RNLI volunteers. Just as we finished our meal we noticed the lifeboat leaving the harbour on a shout. I decided that we ought to go and revisit the station as we knew there would be people there to meet. We introduced ourselves and were made most welcome, not only by crew members but also the younger generation, I can only surmise that they were either relatives of the crew or budding future crew members. It soon became apparent that the coxswain had been told of our project and he sent a message to us asking us to wait for his return as the shout was now cancelled, but I had no Knowledge of why this happened.

When the boat finally arrived back earlier than expected, the crew started trickling in one by one and then the coxswain arrived. He was full of enthusiasm for what we were doing and insisted that we come back in the morning to the station to shower, make coffee, watch the TV, use the phone, with everything on hand for us. He showed us around, making sure that we knew where to find everything in the morning, assuring us that there would be nobody else in the station and then handed us the key, insisting that we promise to return it the next day. We were very appreciative and felt humbled to be trusted with the key to the station. Then we returned to the caravan at the end of our interesting day.

# Day 83, June 23

We were up early in the morning to return to Eyemouth lifeboat station and were surprised to find two men there despite the coxswain saying that there would be nobody there and that we would have the place to ourselves. It turned out they were there to pick up a lifeboat which was sitting in the harbour and take it for repairs. They soon finished their coffee and left us to it. Both Brenda and I made use of the facilities at our disposal before Brenda and I later caught up with Brian who had gone off to the doctors because of his dermatitis. We returned to site and I made ready to scoot to Berwick-upon-Tweed.

In the meantime Brenda and Brian drove there and found the lifeboat station where they met Hazel and Jennifer, two RNLI volunteers, who each gave £5 for the RNLI pot. They were waiting with the crew for my arrival but unfortunately I had misread the map and taken a wrong turning. I knew I had to have a railway line on my left and so I thought I was on track, pardon the pun! It suddenly dawned on me that I was lost on the back roads. My idea had been to avoid a dual carriageway by going round the countryside, but the diversion cost me two hours. I spoke to two men, one of whom was down a hole in the road almost shoulder level with the road surface making some kind of repair. I asked the quickest way back to Berwick-upon-Tweed. Following his instructions, I found myself heading in the right direction and on my way I came upon a field with a boundary of wildflowers, poppies and blue cornflowers, a wonderful sight to see in the countryside! If only this were more widespread throughout the UK, encouraging insects and birds back into our lives as they were many years ago and maybe reducing the need for pesticides. I was wondering whether I should take a photo or continue and try to make up for lost time. In the end I did stop and took a couple of shots very quickly, which turned out to be a mistake as the shots were blurred due to my haste. Also adding to my frustration, were the number of comfort stops I had to make, losing even more time. After phoning Brenda, to warn her that I was going to be very late because I had failed to read the map properly, I carried on through the countryside until I arrived at the A698 leading to Berwick-upon-Tweed. I still faced crossing the A1 dual carriageway which was a particular tricky operation because of the fast moving traffic. After I had succeeded in crossing, I navigated my way through the outskirts of town and eventually arrived at the town centre. There I asked for directions to the lifeboat station and

Me with Hazel at Berwick-upon-Tweed.

was correctly informed how to reach it but, as I continued downhill towards Bridge End, I was told by an ignorant person that I should be on the pavement! I eventually arrived at the bridge and could see on my left the lifeboat station across the river Tweed. When I reached the station I phoned Hazel, one of the volunteers who had been waiting for me. She had returned home by then but had said that when I arrived she would return to the station to meet me. She kept her word. After taking photos, we were then invited into the new station which stands opposite the old one. Over coffee, I apologised for my lateness and told my story of the day. We returned back to the caravan site for dinner. It had been quite an eventful day for me, since I had managed to lose myself, but I must confess I still had enjoyed the ride.

## Day 84, June 24

I woke first and let Sam out of the caravan on his extending lead at the same time making sure that I kept the door almost shut to hide any embarrassment on my part whilst Sam went about his business. It was a sunny start to the day with a chilly wind. After breakfast Brian received a surprise phone call from Motability to say his MOT would run out by the 28th of June, which meant our stay at the next site would have to be for four days. We moved South 49 miles to Broomhill near Amble, a small site which had just an electrical hook up but no showers or toilets. Our run down the coast was an easy-going one, the temperature was 15° and the journey took about an hour and a half. Reaching the site, we found our pitch had our name pinned to a hedgerow and we were advised by other campers to position our caravan parallel to the hedge.

Caravan settled, we drove to Amble to find a chemist. I needed three months supply of medication for my high blood pressure but I found out that I needed to see a doctor, before I could collect my medicine. We found the medical centre in Amble and it wasn't long before I was seen by a friendly female doctor, checking my blood pressure before giving me the prescription I needed. After telling her about our project she kindly wished us well for the rest of our journey. We left the centre and returned to the caravan for our evening meal.

## Day 85, June 25

My trip on the scooter today involved a journey of approximately 18 miles covering three lifeboat stations. During the night we had light rain and a little more in the morning but it soon turned out to be a nice day, with the sun hitting us around 19°. We drove up the coast to Seahouses lifeboat station. During the summer months it is possible to take a boat trip from the harbour out to the Farne Islands to see the spectacular bird islands. It was an experience we had had in 2013 and one I recommend to anyone interested in wildlife. To be up close to nesting birds is quite amazing, but should you decide to make the trip to the islands, especially if you leave the boat and walk around where the birds are nesting, I strongly advise you to wear a hat as the Arctic terns have very sharp pointed beaks and like to attack you by aiming for your head, while protecting their nests sites. Brenda and I, along with my sister and her husband, had visited the islands at the beginning of June, so I recommend you don't leave it too late in the summer for your visit.

Back to the trip. Once again there was nobody at the Seahouses station so it was out with the scooter from the back of Brian's car and off I went down the coast to Craster. I travelled along the B1340 to Beadnell, a small coastal village, before turning right and cutting inland through pleasant countryside until I arrived at a small place called Embleton. There I joined a much smaller road leading to Craster. If you've not been down the North East Coast and have always thought of it as being cold, wet and windy, which to a large extent is probably true, but there are many beautiful places to be discovered along this fantastic coast. I would urge you to pay a visit to this part of the country at least once in your life time and I think you will be pleasantly surprised. A part of the coast I missed while on this trip was the small town of Bamburgh, which has a large and dominant castle standing high on a solid cliff edge overlooking the town on one side and the sea on the other. Just a few hundred yards up the road there is a museum dedicated to Grace Darling who famously rescued nine people from the wreck of the steamship SS Forfarshire in 1838 and became a national hero.

There was nobody on site at Craster and so I continued my journey on what I can only describe as one of those back country roads. In my mind I imagined myself as someone out for a walk enjoying the countryside. After a short stretch I reached the B1339 and in a couple of miles, arrived at the A1068, leading into the ancient town of Warkworth and its Castle. Travelling alongside the River Coquet with its wildlife and on down the High Street, I eventually found the lifeboat station at Amble, just on the edge of town. Apart from my team awaiting for me, there was nobody else around and so we left to shop at the Co-Op and then returned to site.

We were given £5 for the RNLI pot by a couple from a neighbouring caravan. We also soon made friends with a lovely couple who were living in a motorhome; they spend their summers in there RV and then go wintering abroad. Next to their motorhome, was a small tent which housed a washing machine etc. They explained that they always pick sites like the one we were on, whereby you just have an electric hook, with a minimal cost, in this case around £10 per night. In these circumstances you would need to rely on your own chemical toilet with onsite disposable facilities. They had with them two push bikes and a trailer which could be fixed to the back of a bike and which enabled them to tow their dog in the trailer until they reached their destination where they would walk the dog. We finished the day in temperatures occasionally reaching around 21°.

## Day 86, June 26

Today was to be a day off. It turned out to be a nice fine sunny day and we found our way to Druridge Bay. Brenda and Sam went for a paddle along the sandy stretch of beach which goes on for some six miles. Immediately behind it is Druridge Bay Country Park. There I sat and watched them from the top of the sand dunes overlookng the beach surrounded by lots of wildflowers. The way down to the beach from where I was sitting was just too difficult for me to tackle, so I just sat there taking in the view during the hour that I spent in that lovely place. Afterwards we left the beach travelling North and we spotted a poppy field next to the road with a convenient place to stop. We spent something like an hour there taking photos, joined by many other photographers with the same thing in mind. Leaving the poppy field, we stopped at Warkworth Castle but unfortunately weren't able to enter the grounds as the castle was closed at this time of day. We took some photos from the car park before driving into Warkworth town for a look round then returning to site. There we sat outside and chatted to our new friends.

## Day 87, June 27

With breakfast over, we moved our bedding into Brian's end of the caravan as usual, making ready for today's plan. It looked like a sunny day ahead. We drove into Amble to find a launderette and an ATM. Then I left Amble on my way to Newbiggin lifeboat station travelling first on the A1068 until I reached the junction with a signpost to Newbiggin-by-the Sea.

Although we met nobody here, I feel it is important to mention the history of this particular station, for two reasons; firstly this station is the oldest operational boat house in the British Isles and Ireland, and secondly no account could be complete without special reference to the part played by Newbiggin's women. Before the advent of the lifeboat tractor, launching and recovery would be assisted by the women shorehelpers. Their exemplary record was officially recognised by the Institute thanking them, on vellum, in 1927 and again in 1940. In 1927 the lifeboat required the help of 25 women serving the fishing fleet. Most of the regular crew were out in their fishing boats so a scratch crew was put together consisting of miners, who had just come off their shift, but without the help of the women, it would have been impossible to get the lifeboat afloat in the heavy seas. In order to keep the boat straight many waded waist-deep into the surf.

Back to the trip, after finishing their business at Amble, Brenda and Brian returned to the caravan to drop off the washing and kippers, which we were all looking forward to later. They then came to join me at the Newbiggin station but, since there was nobody there and by now it was lunch time, we found a seat on the edge of the beach with good views out to sea to have our sandwiches, making a pleasant change to sitting in the car and keeping out of the rain and wind. After lunch we loaded the scooter into Brian's car to avoid the dual carriageway ahead of us and, missing out Blyth lifeboat station, yet another unmanned station, they dropped me off at a convenient place to continue my scoot to Cullercoats lifeboat station. We now found ourselves in a much busier built-up area but again there was nobody at the station, when we met up again. At least it was an interesting place, close to the River Tyne estuary, with all the local attractions of the nearby harbour and buildings you would expect to find in such a place, but this was just a brief encounter with no time to take everything in.

From here I continued on a short journey down the coast to Tynemouth station which we had contacted previously as this was going to be the 100th lifeboat station we visited. This station has a notable history of bravery with 27 awards for gallantry. The present lifeboat, the Spirit of Northumberland, is named in memory of the first lifeboat station at North Shields which was established over 200 years ago. Again we were welcomed with the usual chat and hot coffee which I needed to warm me through. It was a dry day, but when travelling at eight miles an hour and occasionally hitting ten, the wind can sometimes be very cold, as it was this day. While we were there we watched them on an exercise. Also while we were at the station, the sky blackened and it started to rain, accompanied by thunder and lightning. However, the storm didn't last very long and, when the rain stopped, we said our goodbyes and left to return to the caravan and kippers!

## Day 88, June 28

Brian was up and out by 8:00 am to drive his car to Newcastle for its MOT and service. This left Brenda and me with a free day. After breakfast we drove to Amble and visited the launderette. While waiting for our washing we had a cup of coffee in the harbour near the lifeboat station. After wandering around for some time, we eventually ended up for lunch in a nearby garden cafe, with Sam tucked away in the corner. Lunch over we drove to Alnmouth, a delightful little place about four miles north of Amble. While looking around we had a phone call from Brian to say his car had failed the MOT and needed some welding to be done on the exhaust. This delay meant another night's stay. On our way back Brenda and I stopped off at Warkworth, picked up some fish and chips for us and Brian when he returned to site. Luckily for him he managed to get a lift back to the caravan from someone working at the garage.

## Day 89, June 29

The morning began with a phone call for Brian at eight to say his car would be ready by ten. It was a warm and sunny day and we started to pack up after spending our extra night on site. Brian and I left for Newcastle to collect his car leaving Brenda to add a few more updates and tidy up the caravan ready for the move. We returned to the site and after lunch, lifted the caravan jacks using my battery operated drill. We were ready to leave at around 2:00 pm for a journey of 57 miles. By now the temperature was around 21° and it would have been an ideal scooter day. However we arrived at our new site at Crimdon House Farm, Hartlepool, at around 3:30 pm and had an easy spot to park the caravan. After connecting all the utilities, Brenda and I left Brian with Sam and drove into Hartlepool to top up with diesel and do more shopping.

## Day 90, June 30

It was sunny most of the morning but rain came along later. After breakfast we all drove to Sunderland lifeboat station. The only people there were those working in the shop. After chatting with them I left on my journey of approximately 18 to 20 miles travelling down the coast to Seaham lifeboat station. There I met up with Brenda and Brian and we had our lunch before leaving for Hartlepool lifeboat station. It meant finding my way onto the B432 and then joining the A1086 at Easington. This took me back to the coast and into the built up area of Hartlepool. This is another station which has been in operation for over 200 years. It has two lifeboats; a Trent class and B class Atlantic 75. The crew have been presented with 23 awards for gallantry including one gold medal. We met up and joined Gary, an RNLI volunteer on station, for a cup of coffee and lots of photos taken in the garden where Gary had made a sign in stones representing the RNLI. As far as we were aware the photos were to appear a couple of days later in the local newspaper. Leaving here we returned to site for dinner. Terry our youngest son sent some photos of Abi, his stepdaughter and our newly acquired granddaughter, in her prom dress for us to admire.

## Day 91, July 1

After breakfast we broke camp and left for Whitby some 45 miles down the coast for Long Leas Farm caravan site. We eventually found the site after circling round some narrow roads and managing to turn the caravan round in a car park next to Whitby Abbey. The site was some way away from Whitby itself. Our space was on a slight slope which caused the same problem with backing the caravan into position as before. The site owner had asked us to position the caravan into a space at the top of the slope. Unfortunately while attempting this manoeuvre my car kept stalling. This hadn't happened since Aberystwyth. After many attempts and failing miserably a neighbouring caravanner came to our rescue. He offered to hook up the caravan to his four by four and position the caravan for us, which he did very successfully. Later that day we drove to the car park next to the Abbey. We walked around the path to take a few photos of the views we could capture of the town in the valley below us and the Abbey itself. On our return to the car I managed to slip over on the gravel path and badly grazed my knee. I had to be rescued by Brenda and Brian who got me to my feet again. I managed to walk back to the car like a dog with its tail between its legs. It was a warm and sunny day again and Whitby was absolutely heaving with people. There were many tourists enjoying the holiday atmosphere.

# Day 92, July 2

After getting up and letting Sam out we had breakfast with another really hot day in prospect. We all drove to Redcar where I started my journey for the day. It was another busy place with lots of people around but we found the lifeboat station very easily and managed to park the car close by. We walked in and found some crew members there. After explaining our purpose for being there they took some photos of us to use on their website. Unusually they did not offer us coffee; however, I would have refused it, knowing that I'd soon be looking for yet another comfort stop after leaving them, as I had an approximately 25 mile scoot, taking as much as three hours plus to get back to Whitby.

Leaving Redcar I first travelled along the A1085 and picked up the A174 travelling south to Runswick and Staithes lifeboat station where Brenda and Brian were waiting.

These two lifeboat stations had merged into one. It was hard to find, down the bottom of a very steep hill, and there was nobody on site. We had our lunch there and then Brenda and Brian headed back to Whitby while I continued to travel down the A174 coming inland for a while then turning back towards the coast again. The scenery is spectacular along this road and is a beautiful part of the British coastline. I was climbing and descending fairly steep hills. When going downhill I was totally relying on the braking system built into the electric motor which can seem a little hairy but by now I was well used to it. I had no fear and was at total ease and confident with the scooter. As I approached Whitby, after a spectacular ride I began to realise that I was not going to make it into Whitby.

The scooter was slowing down and something did not feel right. I had not experienced anything like this before, apart from when I was going up very steep hills. I found a convenient place to pull over, luckily into a lay-by, just as the batteries ceased to function. Fortunately I had found a place where it would be easy to get the scooter into Brian's car without blocking part of the road. I needed my backup crew so I checked my phone for a signal and it was fine. I phoned Brenda, explained the problem to her and soon she and Brian returned to rescue me. There was just enough power to load the scooter into Brian's car.

We returned to site where we sat outside the caravan, enjoying our dinner and talking over the events of the day. It was only later that we discovered that Brian hadn't connected all four batteries together! I had therefore exhausted one pair but left the other pair fully charged but out of action. Had I realised the cause of the problem I could have easily rectified it myself. It was always left to Brian to charge the batteries overnight separately and reconnect them the next day. The good thing was that it was easily rectified and had not turned out to be a really major problem.

## Day 93, July 3

It was a stunningly beautiful morning which helped make up for my failure to ride into Whitby the previous day. I decided to return to roughly the same place from where I had had to call Brenda and Brian to pick me up, and to ride into Whitby from there. Those of you who know Whitby know how very crowded it can be as I have mentioned before and this day was no exception. The place was heaving again. The three of us met outside the old lifeboat station, now a museum, and waited there to see if we could collect any money for the pot. I only managed to collect £7.00 of which £5.00 was donated by someone who had read about our trip in their local newspaper. Brenda left me and walked up the road behind the old station where she found a car park with views across the harbour and the town and suggested that we take a couple of photos from this vantage point. Eventually I found the new lifeboat station tucked away through a narrow road on the opposite side of the harbour across the River Esk but, once again, this was an unmanned station. In the afternoon we decided to drive to Grosmont railway station for a trip on the steam train to Pickering, Sam included. Although it was a pleasant journey through the countryside the scenery was largely obscured by trees which took away some of the enjoyment. On our return to Grosmont railway station, roughly six miles from Whitby, we spent some time looking around and taking photos before we returned to the caravan. With the weather still pleasantly warm we sat outside before preparing dinner, then we went on the computer but the dongle which gave us the Internet expired, so we ended the evening watching TV.

## Day 94, July 4

On the move again. With the caravan hooked up and ready to go, we headed down the A171. The temperature was around 20° and with only 27 miles to go, at noon we arrived at Hunmanby, our next site, which was a nice, clean, small site in what I can only describe as a back garden with dog kennels tucked away further down the garden. Brian was nowhere to be seen which left Brenda, me and the owner of the site having to position the caravan on a hard standing. After contacting our son Tony about renewing the dongle, I managed to achieve this on my mobile phone adding another three months of Internet use. The Internet signal was pretty bad on this site – one of my frustrations with Internet and mobile phone companies who make millions of pounds from their customers and yet are unable to provide a decent signal in places, which in my view, should be possible with the technology available to them! Once Brian had rejoined us we had lunch on the site. This was the second time that we had been on a site with dog kennels and where we were the only caravan during our stay. We were also able to access a toilet on the outside of the owner's house which eased the pressure on our morning ablutions. The day ended after a trip to Filey to find a launderette.

## Day 95, July 5

Before leaving the site in the morning we sent a text to our son Terry to wish him a happy birthday. Tony, our other son, had arranged for a Hull and East Riding newspaper to meet us the next day at Bridlington lifeboat station to interview us and take some photos. With the weather once again on our side, we drove up to Scarborough and parked close to the lifeboat station where we immediately met up with their press officer. Scarborough is another one of the oldest stations. It has 35 awards for gallantry but was tainted by tragedy having lost 15 crew members while trying to save lives of others. Once again we had a photo session outside the lifeboat station.

From the station we could see the beach which was packed with people making the best of the weather. After chatting for a while with the press officer, it was time for me to leave and scoot on to Filey lifeboat station. I travelled down the A165 for about six miles along this stretch of coast with its sandy beaches enjoying the sunshine. Arriving at the station I was met by the coxswain who had heard about our project but was unable to invite us into the station as major upgrading work was in progress. Saying goodbye we found a convenient bench overlooking Filey's sandy beach where we had our lunch. I then scooted on to Flamborough lifeboat station, still travelling south on the A165 until it met the B1292 near a small place called Reighton. I headed to the station which is at a secluded spot north-east of Bridlington but there was no one on site, so I and my crew found a cafe to stop for a cuppa before loading the scooter to return to the caravan site. By now the weather was beginning to turn windy and after our meal we settled down to watch the TV as it had started to rain. At least while we had been travelling there, the weather had been kind!

## Day 96, July 6

During the night it rained heavily and disturbed our sleep a little, so we got up late in the morning. The rain had stopped by around 1:30 when I left the site on the scooter on an eight mile trip to Bridlington lifeboat station which should take me approximately an hour. Once there I joined up with Brenda and Brian and we met the coxswain who made us all coffee, sitting outside in front of the station and enjoying our lunch while waiting for the press officer to arrive from the Hull and East Riding newspaper. This seemed to take a long time and before his arrival the sky opened up and we had torrential rain. Fortunately it did not last long. We were struck by how few people there were here which we noticed seemed to be the norm travelling down the East Coast, just with the odd exception. At last the press arrived and took lots of photos for the paper due out that coming Friday. Over the years many medals have been awarded to the crews at Bridlington. Each year a memorial service is held in memory of a great gale which occurred on 10 February 1871 when 70 lives were lost and 30 ships were wrecked. Two of the Institution's lifeboats put out from Bridlington to aid the wrecks plus a similar one not owned by or administered by them (at that time there were many such lifeboats). It appears that the crew of the small lifeboat was exhausted and their place taken by a volunteer crew. Unfortunately the boat, the Harbinger, presented to the Bowman of Bridlington by Count Gustave Batthyany, capsized with the loss of six of her nine crew.

On the way back to the caravan site we stopped off at Hunmanby Gap, where Brenda walked Sam up to the top of cliff overlooking the lovely long sandy beach which stretched out before her. We returned to site and, with the weather being warm and comfortable, we sat outside with a cup of tea before making our way into Filey for an evening meal in the local pub where we talked over the events of the day.

## Day 97, July 7

It was a glorious sunny morning with the temperature settling around 20°. With breakfast behind us we sorted out the caravan ready for a short 18 mile trip to our next location down the coast. We travelled back down the A165 and then onto the B1242 which took us to Skipsea. The Hull and East Riding newspaper phoned to confirm that we would be in their Friday edition. We arrived at Mill Farm Country Park around 12:30 pm and, after settling the caravan on the site and having lunch, we set out for Hornsea to pick up a new gas bottle and some chemicals for the toilet. After this we cooked dinner and, while Brenda and Brian were watching television, I spent the evening studying the map and camping books, looking for future sites.

## Day 98, July 8

When everything was ready we left the site with Brenda by my side on today's 26 mile journey to Elmtree Farm, Holmpton near Withernsea where we were to spend two nights. The temperature was around 17° and it was sunny with occasional showers. As we approached the site I took a right turn, a wrong move on my part, but luckily just down the road was an area where I was able to turn the caravan round at a triangular grassy patch in the middle of a fork in the road. Brian who was following on behind me stopped as I did. I asked him to go ahead and find the exact route into the site but, for some reason, he refused and I lost my temper with him for the first time. In the end Brenda went with him to check out exactly where the site was so that I could make sure I brought the caravan into the site on the right road. They soon returned and told me that I had turned one road too early. The Elmtree Farm site was small and best described as part of a field; however, it was level and I had no problem in settling the caravan into position. Once we had done this we went into town for supplies.

On our return we tried to get an Internet connection but once again found it impossible. Brenda took Sam for a walk along the nearby cliff tops In the meantime while we were sorting things out in the caravan the owner of the site, Mrs Cox, knocked on our window and introduced herself. She told us she would not be charging us for our stay as she was connected through a friend with the RNLI. So once again we were able to add the site money to the RNLI kitty. On the way into the site we had passed a pub, which was literally within walking distance, advertising steak and chips that evening at a very reasonable price. Needless to say we headed there in the evening for our dinner. After an enjoyable meal and a couple of pints we returned to the caravan for the remainder of the evening.

## Day 99, July 9

With the morning chores and breakfast out the way, I left the site on the scooter to travel to Withernsea lifeboat station which was just a short distance from the caravan. On the way there I was approached by a man with a camera who introduced himself as the press officer for the lifeboat station. At the station I was met by a crew member who had opened up the station especially for my arrival. Withernsea is a small station with a D class lifeboat and is normally unmanned. Then the press officer arrived and we spent some time chatting and having photos taken. Brenda and Brian went off into Withernsea to find a launderette, planning to return to the caravan once they had finished there. Meanwhile the crew members and volunteers warned me that I wouldn't be able to get to the Humber lifeboat station on my scooter because the three mile peninsula road was partly covered by thick sand. I was advised to go as far as I could and then load the scooter into the back of Brian's car. This advice made me all the more determined to try to go all the way on the scooter and so I left Withernsea lifeboat station and returned to site, before leaving on a 16 mile journey ahead of Brenda and Brian, to scoot to the Humber lifeboat station.

On this isolated spot there are no fewer than seven families living there permanently. They are the only full-time family crew members employed by the RNLI. The Humber lifeboat station is situated in one of the remotest places around the UK at the end of a long narrow peninsula. This makes travelling at any speed to and fro along the sandy stretch terminating at Spurn Head very difficult. The mouth of the river Humber has some very shallow areas with sand banks just under the water's surface which also make it a particularly dangerous area, in turn giving it an excellent reason for a lifeboat station at Spurn Head especially with the amount of shipping travelling in and out of the major northern port of Hull. On my way there I travelled along some quiet, unclassified, narrow roads slightly inland but following the coast closely with its a long stretches of sandy beaches, part of the Spurn Heritage Coast. I was in no particular hurry and was just enjoying the freedom that the scooter was able to give me. I headed down through Holmpton Hamlet following the road as it turned to the left and headed closer to the sea. I then turned right passing through Out Newton and then moving away from the coast but still following this narrow road until I met with a left turn which I took heading back towards the sea before bearing right and arriving at Easington. I continued my journey on the B1445 passing electricity pylons set within what I can only describe as scrubland with salt tolerant plants growing in between the sand and stones covering the area. This gave me the opportunity to stop and take the odd photo with the weather on my side – so far! I eventually arrived at a pub called the Crown and Anchor in Easington Road situated just before entering the peninsular which leads to Spurn Point, a wildlife protected area. I had arranged to meet Brenda and Brian for lunch in the car park. On my arrival at the pub I could see behind me thick black clouds gathering. While I waited for the others to arrive I got into conversation with a customer from the pub who asked me why I was there and before long I had told her all about our project; she donated £10 to the RNLI. When Brenda and Brian arrived they described the torrential rain they had experienced before they had left Withernsea. They had been sure I would be stuck somewhere soaking wet when they arrived.

I sheltered on the scooter next to them in the car as the rain arrived but fortunately it wasn't that heavy or long-lasting and so I headed off and entered the nature reserve where I was asked for payment, I explained I was on my way to the lifeboat station and was allowed to go through for free as were Brenda and Brian who were following closely behind me. I was determined to scoot the last three difficult miles and arrive at the station on my scooter, avoiding having to load it into Brian's car. In due course I arrived at an area covered in sand which inevitably slowed my journey. Also the road was narrow with few passing places and consequently I had to avoid the few oncoming cars. As I travelled further down the track with Brenda and Brian right behind me I met with a few more complications. I was getting stuck in the sand but twice managed to free myself by manoeuvring the scooter backwards and forwards, trying hard not to have negative thoughts, until I got a grip on the sand and was able to get going again.

Travelling along this narrow stretch one can see the lighthouse at the end of Spurn Point. The earliest reference to a lighthouse here dates from 1427. A lifeboat station was built in 1810 at Spurn Point. Because of its remote location houses for the lifeboat crew and their families were added a few years later. During the First World War two coastal artillery 9.2 inch batteries were installed at either end of Spurn Head. On both sides of the strip of land birdwatchers flock to observe migrating birds throughout the year. Because the sea level here is very shallow, it makes a perfect place for the birds to feed. I eventually arrived at the lifeboat station on the scooter having seemingly done the impossible! I believe I was the first person to have travelled to Spurn Point lifeboat station on a mobility scooter (and probably the last unless you know any different). On our arrival we were met by several members of the RNLI and of course the coxswain who is the man leaning on the front of my scooter in the following picture.

His nickname is Spanish as I believe this probably comes from his Spanish ancestry but don't quote me on that – there must be a clue there somewhere. As Brenda and Brian got out of the car and let Sam out to stretch his legs, we were told that dogs were not allowed in the nature reserve. Apparently at the entrance to the reserve, there had been signs saying just that, but we had all failed to see them. After our initial chat, meeting more of the crew and having our photos taken, we were invited into the station where we sat and had coffee with the crew and coxswain. We chatted for two and a half hours. The coxswain told us that he had been contacted

Us, Spanish the coxwain and crew at Humber lifeboat station.

by the BBC who wanted to establish whether our project was newsworthy. He told them he thought it was but in the end they never contacted us which was a shame because it would have given us nationwide coverage and I'm sure we would have raised more money as a result of it. During our chat with Spanish he told us about some of the other fundraising schemes carried out by people travelling round the coast. He classified us as one of the most eccentric groups he had met doing such a project and I'm proud of that label. Before we left, Spanish showed us a disc that they had made which poked fun at the Skegness lifeboat crew in which their boat was being attacked with bombs etc. He asked us to deliver it to the crew there and so without hesitation we took the disc for delivery. For our journey back to the caravan we loaded the scooter into the van and said our goodbyes. We arrived back at the caravan with fish and chips for our evening meal, after spending one of the most memorable days of the entire trip, thanks to the fantastic RNLI people who do such a brilliant job.

# Day 100, July 10

When we were having breakfast and getting ready for our next move the owner, Mrs Cox, came over for a chat. She suggested that we might like to go to Withernsea as a group of fundraisers were assembling at the lifeboat station there preparing to participate in a bike ride to raise valuable funds for the RNLI. It didn't take any persuading from our point of view so later that morning we went to the station. We were met there by the assistant mayor who, after being introduced to us, made a donation towards our RNLI pot as did the businessman who happened to be there with him. We watched the bike ride get underway; there were three separate distances on the bike ride, the longest was approximately 18 miles. In the first picture they are ready for the off and in the second picture there is a mobility scooter made up to look like a mobility boat but I'm not sure whether it took part in the event. Unfortunately just as the ride got underway one of the younger riders came off his bike and was injured and so was unable to continue.

We were invited back to the village hall in Holmpton where the riders were due to finish their challenge and refreshments were provided. As we entered the car park we could see the village hall was very dated and needed a great deal of repair and it was the same inside, We helped prepare for the arrival of the fundraisers and I ended up showing a gentleman how to fill the urn to make hot water for

Withernsea bike ride.

Withernsea.

the teas and coffees. I was surprised at his lack of experience but probably as a volunteer he may never have had to deal with an urn before. I was only glad I could help. It wasn't long before the first riders started to appear. Tea and coffee were served together with sandwiches, etc. Then more people started to appear, and soon the village hall was filled with the young and not so young, all having a well-earned rest. It remains for me to thank Mrs Cox and all her friends for the warm welcome we were given during our stay there.

When it was time for us to leave, with a 75 mile journey to the next site in front of us, we returned to the caravan. We left the site at approximately 2:15 pm with the temperatures now at 19° and finally arrived at 4:45 at Arklow House Farm, Theddlethorpe near Mablethorpe. It was an easy position on which to park the caravan and we soon had the utilities up and running as it had started to rain. After finishing our evening meal we managed to connect to the Internet sending the usual emails and updates.

# Day 101, July 11

With breakfast over we set off on a warm and sunny morning with temperatures around 21°for Cleethorpes lifeboat station. This is one of seven stations operating a lifeboat funded by viewers of the BBC television programme Blue Peter. The crews have been presented with 10 awards for gallantry, the last being a silver medal in 2004. Cleethorpes was a lovely clean place with a nice promenade. We found the lifeboat station and chatted with the crew over a cup of coffee. Then I left to go to Mablethorpe on an estimated 20 mile journey. I travelled South on the A1031 through very rural countryside passing Saltfleet. For a while the road was much closer to the coast until it took me back inland for some time. Meanwhile Brenda and Brian stayed at Cleethorpes attempting to collect money but the place was very quiet so they did not achieve their objective. They met me en route at around 2:00 pm for lunch and at approximately 2:30 pm I set off again travelling some 12 miles through many small villages before I completed my journey at Mablethorpe lifeboat station. Brenda and Brian had arrived there an hour before me. Once again the station was closed and there seemed to be nobody around in this part of the country, and we wondered if it had been affected by the recession.

## Day 102, July 12

It was a windy day but there was plenty of sunshine. Our son Terry phoned to say his commitments at home were preventing him from making the journey to visit us and, although we were a little disappointed, we understood. Whilst we were preparing for my trip to Skegness I realised that my fleece was missing and came to the conclusion that I had probably left it at one of the lifeboat stations we had visited the day before. I therefore had to carry on with a little less body insulation than normal.

I left at 12 o'clock travelling South again on the main road, the A52. After leaving Maplethorpe I scooted through a built-up seaside area until I reached Sutton on Sea. At this point the road moves away from the coast. I decided not to travel on the unclassified road which follows the coast much more closely because I thought that travelling on main roads would help raise our profile. Sadly this proved to be ineffective on a journey of 16 or 17 miles and I returned to the coast two or three miles before reaching my destination; however, this was a successful ride for me as I passed through rural countryside which I enjoy the most, feeling more relaxed and more able to look round at the environment I was passing through since there were fewer vehicles on the road.

I arrived at Skegness lifeboat station by 2:45 pm. In the meantime Brenda and Brian, having refuelled the car and shopped, also arrived at the station where we were welcomed in by John and other members of the crew. John is seen here with the three of us. There has been an all-weather lifeboat here for over 175 years and over the long history of this station many crew members have received bravery awards. Today it has two lifeboats protecting

Skegness lifeboat station.

one of the region's busiest beaches and the surrounding coast. We handed over the disc given to us by Spanish, the coxswain of the Humber lifeboat station, and while we had coffee with them on went the disc which was followed by a few choice words from John and the crew! Of course they could see the funny side of it. I'm sure that the crew of manned stations must become a little bored at times and this type of tomfoolery would brighten up their days in between the serious work of saving people's lives. When we left the lifeboat station we stayed around for a while to see if we could collect any money and succeeded a little.

Then we returned to site to cook dinner. When I went to pay the owner the £30 for our stay he kindly waived the fee, and it was added to the RNLI pot.

# CHAPTER TWELVE

# East Anglia

## Day 103, July 13

With the caravan safely attached to the car, a chilly breeze blowing and the temperature around 17°, we set off for our next site, an 87 mile journey to Fallowfield Campsite at Burnham Market in Norfolk, where we arrived at 2:15 pm. With practice and a firm routine, setting up all that›s necessary was not taking too long now. We had lunch but finding the mobile and TV signals poor we sat around for a while before deciding to go into Wells-next-the-Sea and look around the harbour.

This was quite an attractive historic town which had until recently been a large producer of malt. We eventually found a road with a high bank along the sea side of the road, leading to a car park at the end of which was the unmanned lifeboat station. Brian and I waited in the car park while Brenda took Sam for a walk along the high bank which supported a tow path back to the town. Then we picked up Brenda and Sam before returning to site where we heard from Leanne, to say there was no sign of her baby yet.

## Day 104, July 14

During the night there was rain and wind and in the morning we received a text from Colin to say that Leanne had started her contractions.

We left the site and drove to Hunstanton lifeboat station. The crew at this station has saved over 460 lives, rescued 10,496 people and educated 494,000 plus children. When we arrived we were met by the manager who lived in a cottage on site. After explaining our presence he opened up the station and allowed us to view the hovercraft, one I believe of only three hovercraft used by the RNLI at stations around the UK. He presented Brenda with a fridge magnet to add to her collection before I left to scoot back to Wells-next-the-Sea. I travelled along the A149 and headed east on a 14 mile journey. As I left Hunstanton, the road runs parallel to the coast between high hedges. Passing close to Burnham Market, the roads forks at a centre green triangle which gives it an attractive appearance with a traditional village atmosphere and all manner of shops making it a village worth exploring. I was unaware of the attractions along this stretch of coast with its small villages and towns on the way, so my ride today was all the more enjoyable.

Arriving at Wells-next-the-Sea, Brian dropped Brenda off so that she could walk Sam along the high bank to the lifeboat station as before. When we arrived, fortunately for us, they were in the process of launching the lifeboat on an exercise. Together with

Hovercraft at Hunstanton.

other members of the public we stood at the side of the station to watch the launch. This gave us a first-class view of them launching the lifeboat using a tractor. In the following picture they are about to launch the boat on the exercise. Later we walked round to the opposite end of the station where we met two crew members. We explained our project to them and were immediately invited in and up to the viewing platform, where we watched the rest of the exercise in comfort and joined the crew for coffee. Wells-next-the-Sea lifeboat station has been established for over 175 years. The crew have been presented with 18 awards for gallantry, but the station has also seen tragedy with 11 crew losing their lives whilst attempting to save others. This makes our project all the more worthwhile, supporting people with great courage in their effort to save lives.

Wells-next-the-Sea lifeboat station on exercise.

## Day 105, July 15

Colin texted to say that Harley had been born in the early hours and also sent us a lovely picture.

This day our journey was 35 miles travelling to our next site, at Stoney Brook Caravan Site, North Walsham. It was a well-kept site on a slight hill with easy parking for the caravan, close to the site facilities. After lunch we left for Sheringham, a town set on a cliff top, to find the lifeboat station. Leaving Brian's car we walked and eventually found the station tucked away right at the end of a promenade. The lady who was looking after the shop there gave us a small donation after we explained our project. We returned to the car, unloaded the scooter and I then left for Cromer lifeboat station. I was still travelling on the A149, a short distance of some four miles to Cromer. After arriving I chatted to the mechanic and got directions to Happisburgh lifeboat station. I left Cromer and travelled another short distance, maybe 2 miles, along the A140 before rejoining the A149 and taking the easy route rather than trying to navigate along the back coastal roads. I travelled through North Walsham village and continued on until I reached the B1159 which took me towards Walcott before I branched right to my destination at Sea Palling Lifeboat. I arrived before Brenda and Brian. The station is situated in a fairly large car park but there was no one on the station or in the general area. I waited for Brenda and Brian to pick me up which seemed like hours but was probably only an hour or so. For the first time I found myself a little bored and so, to fill in time, drove round and round the car park then down the concrete slipway, taking in the view in both directions where the sea was lapping up to the land, just to pass the time, until they arrived to pick me up!

## Day 106, July 16

My 66th birthday. We had planned to take the day off and have a nice lie in and so, with a cup of tea in bed, I opened the birthday cards from all my family and friends, which Brenda had been looking after since before we left on this fantastic journey. At 9:00 am there was a knock on the caravan door and who should be standing there but my right hand man, Jim. Following this surprise, he had a cup of tea with us before he left for the shops. This gave us time to get dressed, etc. He returned with a chocolate cake, wine, beer and a pot plant. Then we all had breakfast and sat chatting, catching up with things back home. It turned out that Jim had driven up to stay with a friend to enable him to visit us and to see how we were all coping. He told us about the fund-raising going on in our local pub in Edenbridge, The Old Eden, where they had held a couple of race nights to boost the pot for the RNLI. I received lots of emails and text messages wishing me a happy birthday. Although we were away from home, this all helped to boost our morale which, speaking for myself, was already high. Jim took us to a local pub for roast dinner and drinks on him – our first roast in 15 weeks! Afterwards it was time for Jim to return home and we thanked him for his kindness which had made the day just that bit more enjoyable.

## Day 107, July 17

The move this day was 43 miles. The temperature was 18° and it was a bit windy. Our destination was Field Farm Fisheries near Beccles in Suffolk and by the time we arrived it had become hot and sunny but this didn't last. After settling the caravan Brenda managed to do some hand washing but then the rain came down hard so the smalls went on the airer to dry in the shower cubicle. We did some updates and banking on the Internet which was working reasonably well; also mobile reception wasn't too bad but the TV reception was terrible. The day ended with lots of rain.

## Day 108, July 18

It rained heavily during the night which was very noisy once again on the caravan roof but by the time we woke and had our first cup of tea, it had stopped. We all left the site in Brian's car heading for Great Yarmouth, where we picked up supplies and stopped for fuel before visiting the lifeboat station but, once again, there was nobody there. We had a look around and managed to collect a small amount of money before I left on my journey to Lowestoft. I avoided the A12 dual carriageway and instead travelled on minor roads for six to seven miles until I reached the lifeboat station. This has 45 awards for gallantry including 39 medals and two gold medals awarded by the RNLI. There I found yet another John on site and chatted with him until we were soon joined by Brenda and Brian. After saying goodbye to John we left and returned back to the site where we enjoyed an hour in sunshine, trying out our new Flip Ultra HD video camera which, with hindsight, we should have purchased at the beginning of the trip. That evening, Brenda spent some time on the Internet and tried to set up an account on YouTube without success.

## Day 109, July 19

It was a sunny start to the day. My mission for the day was to scoot from the site and travel down the B1127 for a relatively short distance of four miles to Southwold. In the meantime Brenda and Brian found a launderette where they spent in Brenda's words, two boring hours doing two loads of washing at the cost of £11 split between the three of us! After this Brenda and Brian joined me in a car park where we sat and had our sandwiches for lunch. Colin had contacted Brenda and thanked her for the money we had sent for Harley's birth.

After lunch I left for Aldeburgh. I doubled back on the A1095 to join the A12 and skirted round the River Blyth. By this longer route

I avoided having to cross from Southwold to Warbleswick on the tiny ferry. I then joined the B1125 and travelled inland slightly through farmland with fields of free range pigs as company on my way to Aldeburgh lifeboat station. In 2006 they celebrated 180 years as a lifeboat station with 15 medals awarded during the station's history up to the year 2000. When Brenda and Brian eventually found the station I was already there. We had coffee with two of the crew members sitting on a wall just outside the station enjoying the sunshine. Both Brenda and I felt that we would like to return to Southwold and Aldeburgh in the future as they both looked interesting places to investigate. Brenda was able to walk Sam before we returned to the site where Brian cooked dinner. That evening Brenda finally managed to sort out YouTube.

## Day 110, July 20

We moved to Grange Farm, Thorpe-le-Soken, near Clacton-on-Sea. It was a nice easy journey of 56 miles, warm and sunny with the temperature at 20°. After settling the caravan in and doing one of the most important jobs, which was sorting out the TV aerial, we managed to get brilliant reception which put Brian and me in Brenda's good books – although mobile reception wasn't so good. After lunch we drove to Walton on the Naze and Frinton on Sea to check out where the lifeboat station was. We returned to the caravan for dinner and settled down for the evening.

# Day 111, July 21

We were all up and out by 11:00 am. We drove to Harwich lifeboat station where we met two crew members and a lady in the shop. We had the usual chat and afterwards I left for Walton and Frinton lifeboat station which I found at the end of Walton pier. There was no one around but near the entrance to the pier there were one or two commercial outlets where we bought a hot doughnut after having our lunch. As we were leaving we noticed the station crew room up a hill opposite the pier and it wasn't long before we were chatting to a volunteer there who took photos of us which he said might appear in the local papers. He suggested to me that I could scoot to Clacton lifeboat station via the long concrete promenade, which was often used to raise money for the RNLI by having sponsored bike rides there. I decided I'd give it a try as it would make a change from travelling on the road and also because it was so close to the sea. To begin with I passed many rows of multicoloured beach huts where the path was much wider than I was to experience later on. When I reached a quieter area the travelling was generally okay but at one point there was a very narrow section where I needed to be particularly careful guiding the scooter through. I had to negotiate a bend with a noticeable drop on either side and it would have been a major disaster had I not navigated it successfully. I decided to go ahead but not without a great deal of apprehension because turning the scooter round in such a narrow space would have been extremely difficult, also there would have been all that time wasted having to head back to find a point where I would be able to rejoin the road. Thankfully I succeeded without any problems, eventually arriving at Clacton and meeting up with Brenda and Brian. We found Clacton to be very quiet. There we were in the middle of July with hardly anyone about. On the sea front it was clean and tidy and generally an attractive area but with nobody at the station and with it being so quiet, there was no chance of us raising any money. So, after telling Brenda and Brian of my scoot along the promenade, we returned to the caravan.

## Day 112, July 22

By now we had been away from home for 16 weeks and, although one part of me wanted to be back there to see my family and friends again, the other part just wanted the project to keep on going because we had found the experience so satisfying and enjoyable. Brenda tried to book a hair appointment locally but they were fully booked. We drove to Colchester where I was dropped off with a short journey ahead of me of about nine miles to West Mersea lifeboat station. From Colchester I followed the B1025 passing on my right an area marked danger zone and travelling through low lying countryside crossing over to what is known as Mersea Island. When I reached the beach I turned right and continued on until I arrived at the lifeboat station. Because of the road system Brenda and Brian had arrived first and were sitting in a nearby café waiting for me to turn up. Since we had brought our lunch with us we sat on a bench overlooking the sea and ate it there.

The scooter was parked next to Brian's car and as we were eating we noticed a man looking at the RNLI stickers and flag on the scooter. We walked over to ask why he was so interested and found out that he was a RNLI volunteer whose curiosity had been aroused. After we explained our purpose he phoned the station officer on his mobile who soon appeared on his bike and he was very pleased to meet us. Shortly after his wife joined us on her bike and they showed us around the lifeboat station. During the 51 years of service at least 150 lives had been saved in over 1,650 service launches. This made West Mersea one of the busiest stations in the British Isles.

They were disappointed that we hadn't warned them in advance of our visit but the problem I always had in making such arrangements was that we, especially I on the scooter, would have been expected to arrive at a lifeboat station at a particular time. Crew members who turned up to greet us would expect us to be there and it would

Us at West Mersea.

put great pressure on us to get from A to B in a set time; we only did this when we felt sure in advance that we could make it. Even then, as at Berwick-upon-Tweed, things could go wrong.

After our encounter at the station we had a wander around and Brenda walked Sam along the beach where he enjoyed a paddle. We also took a few photos of what appeared to be houseboats in varying conditions of repair at the water's edge. On our way back to base we saw a sign for East Mersea and decided to have a look around there before returning to the caravan. A car park was situated right next to the beach and so we didn't have far to travel. Alongside the car park was a fine row of beach huts painted in many pale colours which made a great opportunity for another photo. Before we left we also had an opportunity to devour an ice cream, before stopping off for fish and chips on our way back.

During the night it rained heavily and once again it was difficult to sleep with the noise.

## Day 113, July 23

Today was a relaxing day. We drove about six to eight miles to Little Bromley, a small village north-east of Colchester. Lynda and her husband Simon with their daughter Eloise had arranged to meet us there. They were travelling back from Norwich after their daughter's graduation and were kind enough to treat us to lunch in a quiet country pub. It gave us a chance to catch up with them both; we hadn't seen Lynda since Day 62, June 2, when she left Fort William. After saying our goodbyes and thanking them, we returned to the site and decided to have a walk. Brian and I rode on our scooters and Brenda walked with Sam into Thorpe-le-Soken which has a small shopping area, a few houses and a church. We returned via a short cut back to the caravan across a cornfield next to our site and as it was such a lovely warm evening we decided to have a longer walk around the field, returning later for tea.

## Day 114, July 24

We moved to Burnham Wick Farm near Burnham-on-Crouch, Essex, a journey of about 48 miles. The site was small although the field we were based in was fairly large and close to the farm buildings. Brian did all the utilities before he left for his home in London to collect his road tax and return the next day. Brenda and I decided to drive into town and find a pub which served a roast dinner. As we left the site, who did we pass? Yes, it was Brian who had taken a wrong turn almost immediately on leaving site whilst following his satnav. We pointed him in the right direction to continue his journey and this story became a source of much amusement to us all, although it was nothing unusual for Brian! After our roast dinner Brenda and I walked along the front. It was similar to a promenade built alongside the river Crouch with various shops, pubs and houses along the way. We enjoyed the warm sunny weather and stopped for the inevitable ice cream on the way to the lifeboat station before going back to the site so that Brenda could do some hand washing. Later we returned to the river walk to end a pleasant evening before retiring to bed.

## Day 115, July 25

A nice sunny start to the day. After showers and breakfast we decided we'd tidy up Brian's bed space in time for his return later on in the day. We left the caravan to find a launderette with dryers and afterwards went to the Co-Op at the other end of town for more supplies, later returning to the pub where we had eaten lunch the day before because both the service and meal had been great, We sat outside as we felt more comfortable having Sam by our side as he becomes irritable if somebody approaches us when sitting at a table. Then we returned to the site, put the shopping away and then left again for a walk; me on the scooter with Brenda and Sam by my side. This turned out to be a two and a half hour walk. We started back along the promenade, resting from time to time, and taking in the views overlooking the River Crouch. Again we stopped for an ice cream and generally felt ourselves unwinding. After we had returned to the caravan and had our tea, it wasn't long before Brian returned from his trip with the road tax he had retrieved from his flat in West London, and so all was well!

## Day 116, July 26

We were up and out relatively early for us. There was a chilly wind to welcome me when I left the site on my way to Burnham on Crouch lifeboat station. On my arrival at the station it was empty of crew members; nothing unusual about that, so I left there for my second target of the day, Southend-on-Sea, a place I knew quite well. I headed inland on the B1010 with a railway line and the River Crouch on my left for about six miles until I reached a staggered crossroads. At this point I needed to turn left down an unnamed road travelling south towards Southend. As I did so a car with two occupants drew up alongside me matching my speed and asking inquisitively what I was doing. I could tell by their speech that they were probably a couple of travellers. After explaining the reason for my being there they seemed delighted to hear it, wished me good luck and then drove on about their business. I continued across the river, down through Ashingdon, then through a more built up area, still travelling south but with more traffic the closer I got to Southend. I worked my way through the busy streets until I found myself in familiar surroundings and eventually on the A13 where I turned left heading towards the pier. In the meantime Brenda had been able to walk Sam for half an hour along the River estuary at Burnham-On-Crouch before arriving with Brian at Southend and finding it very difficult to park. Eventually we all met up.

As we approached the pier we came across a group of 12 senior citizens sitting down and enjoying a chat. They became curious as to what we were doing and when they found out, it wasn't long before they had all contributed to the RNLI pot. We thanked them and continued with our mission. The lifeboat station is situated close to the entrance of the pier but again there was nobody on site. Brian and I decided that we would travel along the mile long pier to the shop at the end which is run by RNLI volunteers. Brian took the pier's mini train and I used the scooter. We left Brenda with Sam behind where they could overlook the pier, waiting patiently for us. After returning to the car and loading the scooter we headed back to the caravan, where Brenda and I prepared the evening meal. The next day was going to see us on even more familiar territory.

# CHAPTER THIRTEEN

# South East

## Day 117, July 27

This day our journey was approximately 97 miles. The temperature was 18° as we drove to Nethercourt Touring Park in Ramsgate, Kent – our home county. The site we had booked was flat which made it easy to park the caravan; the site was clean and tidy but a little bit expensive and, unfortunately, no discount but it was easy to find and convenient for this part of our operation. We soon sorted ourselves out and had our sandwiches. We contacted Brenda's parents and then went on the computer to send some emails. Also Brenda managed to do an upload to YouTube for the first time, filming me on the scooter.

Later we drove into Ramsgate, had a look round and found the lifeboat station, unmanned again. We then returned to the site, cooked an enjoyable dinner and afterwards sent a photo to our local free newspaper in Edenbridge.

# Day 118, July 28

This morning we drove to Ramsgate to find a hairdresser for Brenda to book an appointment. Having done this we left for Sheerness lifeboat station. This station operates a Trent class lifeboat and an inshore D class lifeboat. In its 35 year history the lifeboat crews have been presented with 14 awards for gallantry. I had managed to contact Robin, the coxswain, to let him know in advance of our arrival. Sheerness Docks are in a secure area which meant that we would have to go through security in order to get to the lifeboat station. Sure enough when we arrived there we were stopped at the gates and questioned about our business. After telling security of our mission, they phoned through to Robin and he confirmed that we were expected. One-day passes were issued to each of us, the barriers were lifted and on we went to the lifeboat station after being warned that we could not take photos other than of the lifeboat station itself. Robin was waiting there to greet us but when we got out of the car with Sam Robin informed us that dogs were not allowed in the docks and so Sam was quickly put back in the car out of sight. The reason he hadn't been spotted in Brian's car at the check point was because he was asleep in the front foot well below my legs. Fortunately Sam didn't respond to the sounds made by the security men at the gates because his hearing was failing due to his age. In case you're wondering he was around 17 years old at that time.

Robin invited us into the station where we had our lunch and coffee with him. He explained more about the docks to us, mentioning in particular the arrival of oil tankers etc which is why there is so much security there. When it was time for us to leave Robin presented us with £20 for the RNLI pot and we again passed through security without Sam being detected.

Once we had cleared the A249 and reached the A2, I was dropped off to scoot to Whitstable. I headed towards Faversham and then travelled on back roads turning left at Love Lane on through to Seasalter and Whitstable

It was a pleasant journey with occasional glimpses through hedges at the fields on either side of the road until I met the sea wall on my left before arriving at Whitstable. As usual Brenda and Brian were already at the lifeboat station waiting for me and although the shop was open there appeared to be no crew members on site. We decided to spend some time there since the weather was good and there were plenty of people milling around. We spotted a camera crew filming the comedian, Adrian Edmonson, and we waited for an opportunity to approach him but alas, this did not happen. By 6:30 pm we decided to return to the caravan feeling a little disappointed. Brenda uploaded clips to YouTube, ending quite an eventful day.

## Day 119, July 29

I left the site this morning to scoot into Margate travelling through the busy streets until I found the lifeboat station which is to the side of the Turner Contemporary building. There I met up with Brenda and Brian. Once again we were welcomed into the station which has celebrated some 150 years of existence. The crew have received ten awards for gallantry but it has also seen tragedy with ten crew members losing their lives saving others at sea.

By one o'clock I had left for Ramsgate Lifeboat Station, keeping to the coast road which took me uphill at first and then levelled off. I stayed as close as possible to the coast passing the Winter Gardens and the Lido Leisure Centre along the B2052. At the end of Queen Elizabeth Avenue at the roundabout turning left, and joined the B2052, and headed back down to the coast. As I scooted past some houses I received a small donation from a man cleaning his car, whose curiosity had been aroused by seeing my scooter with its tall flag mast and the RNLI flag at the very top. I continued through Broadstairs overlooking Viking Bay at this attractive town and beach.

Finally I arrived at Ramsgate yacht marina where once again the three of us met up. Again we found crew members at the lifeboat station and had our lunch with them. It was often difficult for Brian to find a parking space near to the lifeboat stations but on occasions Brian was invited to park in the spaces provided for crew members. After our visit, our last target for the day was Walmer lifeboat station. I left Ramsgate and eventually found my way onto the A256 and travelled through Sandwich and Pegwell Bay National Nature Reserve, eventually turning left and following the signs to Deal. There I scooted west along the promenade, passing a fair that was in full swing with people enjoying the late afternoon sun. I finally reached Walmer lifeboat station. Walmer celebrates over 150 years in service, with 25 awards for gallantry. It was again unmanned but two volunteers had been informed of our arrival, Brenda and Brian arriving at 4:30 pm and I at 5:00 pm. After chatting with the manager and his assistant, they donated £15 for the RNLI pot. After leaving them we went on to a local fish-and-chip shop for our supper, sitting outside the shop watching the world go by. Back to the caravan for the evening, ending a pleasant day's drive for me.

## Day 120, July 30

Leaving the site to day we to drove to Walmer where I was dropped off with the scooter to travel down to Dover lifeboat station. Dover lifeboat station operates a class VII lifeboat which was the biggest in the fleet at this time. The lifeboat station has been in operation for over 165 years with 30 awards for gallantry. I passed by Walmer Castle and Gardens which is run by English Heritage and is well worth a visit. I travelled along the A258 until I reached the A2 Jubilee Way which took me into Dover. Although the journey was largely uneventful, I was extremely apprehensive about my approach to Dover Harbour from the east as I had to travel down the steep hill on an elevated twisty section. I was also concerned about all the heavy goods vehicles which were passing me. I can only imagine some of the things the drivers might be saying to themselves as they overtook me! Once down at sea level I turned left on to Marine Parade, and eventually arrived at the lifeboat station around midday to discover they were having an open day. Since Brenda and Brian had gone ahead of me, I was welcomed with applause from crew members and volunteers, and also a few members of the public. Photos were taken for their website.

While there, we were invited on board the lifeboat, as were the public, but the step up to the boat was too much for Brian and me. I had lost my fleece some time back, but was unaware at which

Dover lifeboat station.

lifeboat station and so I bought one from the shop to replace it and was kindly given a discount.

Just as we were leaving in the car to return to our site at Ramsgate, our son Tony and his fiancée and their dogs arrived which was a real surprise. They had been tracking us via GPS on our mobiles! We all returned to our caravan site to give the dogs a brief walk and then we dropped Brenda in Ramsgate for her hair appointment. The rest of us went to a nearby fundraising event, nothing to do with the RNLI, but even so we managed to collect a small amount of money for it there anyway. After Brenda's appointment we drove to a pub, sat in the garden with the dogs and enjoyed the sunny weather. At around 7:30 pm Tony and Laura left for home, leaving us to return to the caravan after a very happy day!

## Day 121, July 31

We got up, showered, had breakfast and cleaned up, in preparation for the arrival of my sister Ann and her husband Ray. They arrived at 11 o'clock and after a cup of tea and a chat, catching up with their news and they with ours, we decided to go to last night's pub, the Sportsman, for a roast dinner. We returned to Ramsgate for a walk round with our cameras. I noticed a painting on a wall near the harbour, thought to myself how appropriate it was to our project and so decided to include it in this book.

We then returned to the site for sandwiches and cake. After watching the news we decided to go out again to take more photographs and to enjoy the pleasantly warm evening. After this we went back to the caravan for coffee before Ann and Ray set off for home with the promise of a meal at their place the next day in Tenterden.

Ramsgate painting.

# Day 122, Aug 1

As I travelled down the south coast towards our final target at Poole, I was beginning to experience those sad feelings one gets when a project, which had taken years to organize and months actually to achieve, was soon coming to an end.

We left the site late morning with temperatures around 25° and a journey of 55 miles to Peasmarsh near Rye in East Sussex. The site was situated at the back of a pub called the Cock Inn. While settling the caravan on site I received a phone call, arranged by my son Tony, from Meridian Television suggesting they meet us the next day at 11:00 am at Littlestone-on-Sea lifeboat station. This was good news as it would help with publicity and perhaps also raise funds for the RNLI. After lunch we drove to Tenterden and joined my sister Ann and her husband Ray. First we went shopping in Tesco to top up our supplies and then returned to their house where we showered and then sat down with them to enjoy cottage pie and veg for lunch. Our dog Sam seemed a little more at ease because he was now in familiar territory as he would always come with us when we were visiting. Tenterden is an ancient Kentish town with wide pavements and green spaces on either side of the main road. It is a popular tourist town and has the Kent and East Sussex Railway steam train which runs from Tenterden to Bodiam. After spending the evening with the family, we returned to the caravan to prepare for the next day's meeting with Meridian television.

## Day 123, Aug 2

We were up early in the morning. There was a little rain but it was warm and humid and we had a feeling of anticipation about the pre-arranged meeting with Meridian Television. However, whilst travelling down to Littlestone-on-Sea lifeboat station for the meeting I received a phone call from them cancelling the interview. They explained that there had been two murders in their area which took priority over our arrangement and they did not have enough resources to include our story. Of course we were very disappointed as this meant reduced publicity at a vital time coming towards the end of the trip.

We continued on to the lifeboat station which was unmanned and so we just stopped to let Sam stretch his legs. At this point I parted with Brenda and Brian and continued on my journey on the scooter to Dungeness. I followed the coast and the Romney-Hythe and Dymchurch Light Railway line which has a station and cafe near the power station.

At Dungeness lifeboat station, Brenda and Brian were waiting for me, having informed the crew of my pending arrival. Once there I was introduced to the coxswain and a crew member, who made us very welcome with a cup of coffee. Dungeness was one of the first stations to receive the RNLI Shannon class lifeboat on May 31, 2014. She was named Morrell by HRH the Princess Royal. The station has a rich history and in 1940 the Dungeness lifeboat was one of 19 that took part in the evacuation of the Allied troops from Dunkirk. In the 1950s the station was famous for its launches by local women who helped haul the lifeboat down to the sea and haul her back up again on her return to the station. In their yard they had an experimental jet boat, the Mark 1, but this design was no longer being progressed, the Mark 2 being developed instead. This Shannon-class jet boat was launched from the station on Friday the 31st of February 2014 and was first of its kind.

Dungeness is Britain's only so-called desert because of the sparse plants which grow on the pebbly beach; however the area has a rich variety of wildlife and was once a thriving fishing centre. Now it is a great place for photography with the old wrecked boats and fishermen's huts that can be found scattered along the beach not far from the old lighthouse, which is open to the public for those with a head for heights. Close by is Dungeness nuclear power station.

After leaving the station I continued on my journey along the coast back to New Romney again following the A259 again with Walland Marsh on my left, a protected area of special scientific interest. When I finally arrived at Rye Harbour I was met, not only by Brenda and Brian, but also by my sister Ann and brother-in-law Raymond, with his parents and a neighbour. They presented us with £54.20 between them for the RNLI. We sat chatting and enjoying a drink outside the pub opposite the lifeboat station, again this was unmanned, returning to the caravan at the end of an enjoyable day despite missing out on Meridian Television.

# CHAPTER FOURTEEN

# South Coast

## Day 124, Aug 3

Moving to Pevensey Bay today was a relatively short journey of 28 miles to a site at Stone Cross Nurseries. The temperature was around 27°. The site owner directed us to our position which once again was a flat grassy area, nice and easy to park on. After a lengthy chat with the site owner she kindly returned the £36 charge for the three nights we had booked, and we added it to the RNLI pot. After lunch we sat outside the caravan for most of the afternoon, taking care of our washing and other little jobs which needed attention.

Later we drove to Pevensey Bay where our friend Jenny lives. She used to be the landlady of the King and Queen pub in the centre of Edenbridge. When our regular pub changed to new management with no experience of running a pub, we needed to look elsewhere for our Wednesday nights mid-week break and so we decided to try the King and Queen further up the road where Jenny welcomed us. She always saved us a seat, there was always cheese and biscuits for us to share, and she generally spent the evening with us, which made for a great evening out. When Jenny retired she moved from Edenbridge to the coast and Wednesday nights never seemed quite the same again. Today, we were able to spend a happy couple of hours chatting with Jenny, catching up on her news of the new fellow in her life, while we told her all about our journey round the UK.

## Day 125, Aug 4

It was raining hard when we awoke and was still raining when we left for Hastings. Brian dropped me off outside Hastings so that I could scoot to the lifeboat station and then continue my journey further along the coast. I decided to try out the cloak which had been donated by Days Healthcare, the people who supplied the scooter; however I did not realise that it wasn't waterproof!

Once on the scooter I drove into Hastings in the pouring rain and arriving at the station with the cloak wet on the outside but not getting to my clothes on the inside. I was met by my sister, her husband, their neighbour and a couple of her daughters with their children. They were all standing out in the rain waiting for me to arrive. This was a great surprise to me but unfortunately they all got soaking wet. Then we were welcomed into the lifeboat station, the children were shown around and we all had a hot cup of coffee and a great chat with the crew. Hastings lifeboat station, established in

1858, is another of the 19 stations which took part in the evacuation of our forces at Dunkirk to its credit with 30 awards for gallantry. During the Second World War the lifeboat was launched 48 times and rescued 21 lives. One final note of interest in the year of my birth 1944 on the seventeenth of November, searching for a landing craft in very rough seas, the lifeboat capsized. The coxswain and two other crew members were washed out of the boat but all three were rescued. It is also where we first met the guys from Greenmeanie, the company that created our website, Scoot4life.

My journey to Sovereign Harbour lifeboat station just outside Eastbourne, still wearing the cloak but unaware that it really was not waterproof. It was still raining hard as I travelled through

Eastbourne lifeboat station.

Bexhill and I was sticking tightly to the coast along the back roads and crossing the railway line as I approached Pevensey Bay. I was now completely soaked through to my skin as I made my way to Eastbourne Marina where the lifeboat station is situated. The station at Eastbourne was established in 1822, two years before the Royal National Lifeboat Institute itself was founded, and celebrated over 180 years of service. It too took part in rescuing our forces from Dunkirk in 1940 and has 10 medals for gallantry. By the time I arrived there and met up with Brenda and Brian, I was not only soaked to my skin, but I was beginning to shiver as the cold was getting through to my body. It wasn't long before the guys on station noticed our presence and invited us into the station where I was able to warm up. It was not one of my best days.

## Day 126, Aug 5

The sunny weather returned. Brenda and Brian dropped me off at Sovereign Harbour from where I left for Newhaven continuing along the coast on the B2103 again. This took me along the front of Eastbourne parallel to the promenade then rising up the hill to Holywell. Here is the beginning of the South Downs Way which goes all the way to Chichester. I climbed up the zigzagging road through a wooded area and, at the top, joined the road that leads back down to Eastbourne. I continued climbing until I reached the left turn for Beachy Head. From here you can look back down the hill to Eastbourne spread out in all its glory beneath you. I passed the Beachy Head Countryside Centre and pub and then descended towards the famous Belle Tout Lighthouse now a quirky B&B. Here my eyes were presented with a fantastic view overlooking this particular part of the south coast. The road snaked down the hill eventually reaching Birling Gap, and then headed on to East Dean. Many of the buildings there incorporate flintstone in their construction, including the church and the surrounding walls, which make up this beautiful tiny village. It also has a pub at its heart, the Tiger Inn.

With the village behind me, I turned left onto the A259 still climbing uphill. Eventually the road began to level off just after St Mary's Church and the small pond on the left. I then began the descent down to the Seven Sisters Country Park whilst overlooking the spectacular Cuckmere Valley with the Cuckmere River winding its way to the sea. At the bottom of the hill I passed the Country Park, before finally arriving at Seaford. This whole area is of outstanding natural beauty and well worth a visit. Nearby is Alfriston village, a very popular and attractive place. If you approach it from the Seaford side and climb the hill to the car park at High and Over, just a short walk through to your right you will come across a spectacular view, and you will be standing directly above the Litlington White Horse carved into Chalk Hill. Although nearing the end of this fantastic journey, I had been looking forward to being here and hoping that this part of my journey would be a special day for me as this area of the south coast is one of my favourite spots. The weather was good and I was feeling good too knowing just how lucky I was!

On reaching Seaford I met Brenda and Brian for lunch. We sat overlooking the sea whilst having our sandwiches before going on to Newhaven lifeboat station. I rejoined the main road and after passing under the railway bridge we turned left. Just few hundred yards along the road there is a car park, from where it is possible to walk through to the ruins of an old tide mill. Nearby on the sea front are also the remains of what was once part of a hospital ward and nursing home connected to Chailey Heritage known as Tidemills. It was thought that fresh air would aid the recovery of the disabled children who were hospitalised there. At the outbreak of World War II it was abandoned since it was feared that Hitler's forces might land anywhere along the south coast.

I continued to scoot on to Newhaven lifeboat station and I was surprised to be met there by my son Tony and his fiancée Laura. We checked into the lifeboat station where we met the coxswain along with some volunteers. One of the volunteers, a lady, offered to meet us later at Brighton Marina where the Brighton lifeboat station is situated, our next and last target of the day. After a walk along the edge of the river Ouse and taking a few pictures, I set off once again along the coast, this time for Brighton.

I'm ashamed to say that my journey into Brighton was where I met the most abuse that I received on the whole journey, on more or less home territory. The problem I had was with having to drive on the outside of a bus lane, as mobility scooters have to abide by the Highway code that is set out for cars etc. Consequently I had cars and buses passing either side of me; the reason for the abuse was the ignorance of other drivers of the law regarding grade 3 mobility scooters' right to travel on the road! It became clear that I needed to get out of this predicament and move onto the pavement, which I did as soon as I was able, reducing my speed to four mph for my own safety and that of others. At least I had a pavement to ride along here!

I eventually arrived at the Marina where I met up again with Tony and Laura, and Brenda and Brian. Whilst waiting for the RNLI volunteer who was going to open up the station for our benefit we sat in a pub and had a drink. Again this was yet another unmanned station. Although I don't visit Brighton very often these days, mainly due to parking restrictions, it always reminds me of a time many years ago when as a young lad a couple of friends and I decided to spend the weekend there and sleep overnight on the beach. During the early hours of the morning we still had not found a resting place. We got talking to a young local man as to where would be the best place to sleep and after a while he suggested that we came back with him to the room he rented. He warned us that we would have to be very quiet and so as not to disturb his landlady as his agreement stated that he was not allowed overnight visitors. We accepted his offer and crept quietly into his flat and slept in chairs and on the floor. By morning we were all waiting to use the loo. With so many people wanting the loo at the same time, it could have given away the fact that our friend was not alone. Solving this first problem, we then spent the whole morning trying to decide how to get out of the flat without getting our friend into trouble. Eventually we came up with the solution and decided that my friend Laurence would pretend to be his brother, with his brother's friends and that we had arrived in the early hours of the morning to visit him. He told his landlady this and luckily she accepted his explanation. We were able to leave his flat by early afternoon but had missed out on a good part of the day. We never saw this guy again but always wonder what his landlady really made of it all.

Tony and Laura left for home while we were shown round the station and then we returned to our site picking up fish and chips for our evening meal. Later in the evening my sister Ann and her neighbour arrived to collect our washing to take home and return to us later on our journey.

# Day 127, Aug 6

The next site I had chosen was Ellscott Park, Birdham, a small place south of Chichester. I booked the site for four nights to cover the next stretch of coast finishing this leg at Portsmouth. We travelled some 56 miles with the temperature around 22°. We met really heavy traffic and didn't arrive until 1:45 pm. It was a crowded site but level and easy to park. We had obtained a large RNLI flag which we draped over the front of the caravan when on site, together with a bucket to collect money in the hope that people would contribute. This became part of our everyday routine. We met a German couple and their son here who were visiting lifeboat stations in this part of the UK. They told us that there was a similar organisation in Germany and they often spent their holidays in the UK visiting our lifeboat stations. They left us with a small pamphlet in German.

We had lunch but by this time it was raining and so we sat in the caravan checking our emails and doing our Internet banking. When the rain had stopped we drove into Chichester to find a supermarket for more supplies, eventually returning to the caravan to cook our evening meal. This was delayed since we had run out of gas and needed to change the cylinders which proved somewhat difficult but eventually we managed to work out how it was done, leaving us with a late dinner.

# Day 127, Aug 7

Today was Brenda's father's 88th birthday and so she phoned him to wish him a happy birthday. She also phoned Colin to wish his son Maddox, our unofficial grandson, a happy second birthday. It had stopped raining but it was still windy; however it wasn't long before we were blessed with warm sunshine. We drove to Selsey to check out the lifeboat station. We found it very busy as they had an open day in progress and parking was a nightmare. So we drove on to Chichester where we walked along the canal, stopping for coffee and cake in the cafe next to the moorings for the canal boats. Leaving there we drove to a side road that ended facing the canal where was a footpath alongside the canal which we took for a short while enjoying the peacefulness and the surrounding nature. We eventually returned to the caravan for dinner after which we drove to Bosham where my cousin Sue and her husband Chris lived. We spent some time with them having another catch up. Bosham village is situated by a natural harbour which the Romans took advantage of (nearby can be found Fishbourne Roman Palace). It is a beautiful village with its Saxon church standing proud next to the Mill Stream and the National Trust owned Bosham Quay Meadow. Pubs, coffee houses, shops and side streets makes this a very pleasant place to visit.

# Day 128, Aug 8

The sun was coming and going in between the clouds when we left the site to travel through busy traffic to Shoreham lifeboat station. This brand new station is situated in the narrow estuary of the river Adur. We went in and talked to the volunteers in the shop, explaining our mission to them. They kindly took us up in the lift to the area which overlooks the lifeboat. According to my RNLI rescue map it is a Tyne class (this boat may have been upgraded). After a very enthusiastic volunteer explained more detail about the boat and the station, we returned to the car where we sat and had our lunch. I left at around 1:30 pm to travel to Littlehampton lifeboat station. I kept to the A259 and travelled along the coast through Worthing following the beach road before turning off through an area called Ferring which took me back onto the A259. I turned left and followed the A259 until I came across signs that led me through Littlehampton to the lifeboat station. I arrived about 3:30 pm and was met by my sister Ann, her husband Ray and two of her neighbours, Win and Carol, together with our washing. The station although unmanned was open to the public to view their class B (Atlantic 21,75,85) and class D boats. A volunteer kept an eye on the station whilst it was open. We sat outside a cafe, just a short walk away, to relax over a coffee. We noticed a man I guess whose age was between 50 and 60 and of a character that I can only describe as eccentric. He was putting on a display, making a complete fool of himself, that was impossible not to notice. After this we all took a leisurely and enjoyable walk back to the car park alongside the river. Pleasure boats were moving up and down the river and wildlife was accepting the challenge of living alongside human beings. Later we went for a meal in a restaurant on the sea front and eventually we all left and went our separate ways home.

## Day 129, Aug 9

We heard again about the terrible riots in London including Ealing, West London, which is where Brian lives. Fortunately his home was unaffected. Tony phoned for a catch up this morning before we left the site to travel to Selsey lifeboat station. This picture, shows the station and, with the right conditions as mentioned previously, I think makes a good photo. This time parking was not a problem. The shop was open and the ladies there told us that the coxswain was in the lifeboat station. We climbed the stairs onto the gantry and walked over to the station where we spent a short time chatting to the coxswain. The station was established here in 1861 and many bronze and silver medals have been awarded to the crews. In 2011, the year of our visit, the station celebrated 150 years existence.

Selsey lifeboat station.

I left at midday to travel to Hayling Island lifeboat station on a journey which would take me almost four hours. Earlier on we had received an email from the station asking us to notify them of the intended day of our arrival so that they could be there to greet us. Before Brenda and Brian left Selsey they had lunch and gave Sam a walk along the beach. They then left for Hayling Island to await my arrival. On my scooter I travelled along the A286 turning off at the sign to Dell Quay then, after a short distance, I turned right to follow the road leading to the A259 again. I stopped for lunch underneath a fig tree at the entrance of a private house. While sitting there eating my lunch a car drove from the house and stopped beside me. The lady driver, who I assumed was the owner of the house, encouraged me to help myself to the figs which were mostly eaten by wasps, before she left to go about her business.

I was familiar with most of the journey as in the past, when the children were young, we had had a small caravan which I occasionally towed to a campsite at Birdham called Redhouse. This would have been my first choice of a site, but unfortunately it was fully booked. My navigational skills were called on when I arrived at Havant in order to avoid the A27 dual carriageway. I continued on the A259 which overlooked Chichester Harbour through Southbourne, en route passing one of the seven caravan outlets for Chichester caravans who were sponsoring us. I picked my way through the back roads of Havant before crossing under the A27 on a rather large roundabout. From there I was able to pick up the A3023 which led me to the southernmost part of South Hayling seafront with the usual seaside attractions. I turned left and eventually arrived at the lifeboat station, where I met Dee and other volunteers. For me this was one of those especially interesting journeys on the scooter, passing along roads which I would never have normally visited. Hayling Island lifeboat station was opened in 1865. The crew have received three bronze medals along with seven silver medals and other recognitions for their bravery. It wasn't long before I was drinking the usual coffee and been made very welcome.

Before we left, Dee phoned through to Portsmouth lifeboat station, our next call, informing them of our planned arrival later that afternoon. I decided that travelling there on the scooter would be almost impossible. This was because I needed to avoid the dual carriageway system and, because it was getting fairly late, it would probably have taken me many hours navigating my way through the smaller roads. We therefore loaded the scooter into Brian's car and set off for Portsmouth lifeboat station. Arriving there we were welcomed in and sat with two volunteers having more coffee and looking through lots of historical photographs. These were of past members and rescues performed by the brave volunteers of the station, risking their lives to save others. I have to say it was also partly for my own satisfaction to visit all these wonderful places around the coast of the UK. On our return to the caravan we stopped in a pub along the A259 not far from the Chichester Caravans site I mentioned earlier. At that time there were four in the south of England, and three in the Birmingham area. We had our evening meal there before returning to the caravan.

## Day 130, Aug 10

This was to be our last move. A journey of about 55 miles with temperatures around 22° but it was quite windy and the traffic was busy. We eventually arrived at Harts Lodge, Everton near Milford on Sea from where we had four more stations to visit. After we settled the caravan in a quiet corner of the site close to a hedgerow it was time for lunch. We decided to drive into Christchurch and have a walk around with our cameras. It was a place that Brian had never visited. If you've not been to Christchurch then I can highly recommend it. It is a much sought-after place to live with a fine church, set in an area of great beauty. The town's harbour, beaches, nature reserve and historically important buildings make it very popular place for tourists.

## Day 131, Aug 11

We woke to rain in the morning and so I decided not to visit any lifeboat stations that day. We had a fry-up for breakfast and, after putting everything away, Brenda did some updates on the computer. As for me, there was no more looking through our camping books for the next site, which at times had been very stressful. After lunch we left the caravan for Milford on Sea, where Brenda walked Sam and we had an ice cream, before driving along the coast a little and stopping to take the odd photo. We settled for a cream tea and drove into Lymington where we topped up with diesel. Finally returning to the caravan for dinner.

## Day 132, Aug 12

Now, with the finishing line well in our sights, we were up early and drove through the New Forest to Calshot lifeboat station. There we introduced ourselves to quite a few volunteers, no less than 10 to be precise as one had to take the picture you see. After we explained why we were there, we were invited into the station where we talked to the crew about our adventure. Here again we experienced warmth and enthusiasm from the volunteers. Before we left they invited us onto the steps of the station where this photograph was taken.

Calshot lifeboat station.

Calshot lifeboat station has a relatively short history. It was established on 25th July 1970 at an old military flying-boat station and many of the hangers are still there. Also can be seen there is the artillery fort built by Henry VIII to defend the sea passage to Southampton which is currently maintained by English Heritage. Calshot is one of those places along the south coast which none of us had visited before. You can look across to the Isle of Wight and watch the shipping going into Southampton docks etc. It is well worth a visit if you are ever in the area and a great place to stop for a picnic on a warm summer's day. Tony phoned to say that he had been in contact with Meridian Television who were going to meet us at the end of our journey at the RNLI Headquarters and Training College and HQ in Poole. Incidentally the public can enjoy a meal there as well as obtain overnight accommodation.

I left Calshot and travelled back through the New Forest, something which I was looking forward to, on my way to Lymington lifeboat station. As I travelled through the forest with the wild ponies scattered around me I experienced a feeling of freedom which I'm sure is the same that walkers have as they stroll through the countryside, especially with the weather in a kindly mood. Both Brenda and I have visited the New Forest in the past spending time with friends and family camping so we were familiar with the relaxed atmosphere that the forest offers to its visitors.

From Calshot I travelled along the B3053 through Fawley picking up a back road which took me to a place called Hill Top where I joined the B3054. This took me through Beaulieu where the National Motor Museum and Palace House are located. I was soaking up my surroundings as I travelled down to Lymington. Although there was nobody on station when I arrived, the shop was open and a lady volunteer gave us £5 for the pot. We had our lunch there. Lymington is popular with tourists and has a ferry service to the Isle of Wight. It was very busy when I arrived and so we stayed for a while hoping to add to the RNLI pot.

I then journeyed to Mudeford lifeboat station on the A337. As usual Brenda and Brian had gone ahead of me to await my arrival so that, if there was anyone on site, they could explain our purpose in being there. Mudeford is an unmanned station and there was nobody on site and so, after a coffee in a nearby cafe, we stayed a while hoping to collect a little more money for the pot, before we went for a beer. With the scooter loaded safely in the back of the car we drove back to Lymington for fish and chips to round off the day and then returned to our site. This was a private site where we met a couple who travelled around staying at reasonably priced sites with electrical hook-ups, living a relaxing way of life in their retirement and travelling abroad for the winter. This was much the same lifestyle as lived by the people we had met when staying near Amble in Northumberland. I think I would enjoy that way of life if I were fit and had no obligations at home.

# The Final Day

## Day 133, Aug 13

After a cooked breakfast we left the site around midday and travelled to the edge of Bournemouth. There we unloaded the scooter from Brian's car and tied some balloons onto the back ready for my journey to the final lifeboat station at Poole. Poole is a naturally shallow harbour and is a very popular place – particularly with millionaires living along Sandbanks with views of the harbour on one side and its own sandy beach on the other. Brownsea Island is situated almost centrally in the harbour. It is owned by the National Trust and famous as the place where Baden Powell formed the Scouts Movement.

The station was fully aware of our pending arrival with Meridian Television and a full lifeboat crew waiting for me. After a brief navigational error I was soon heading in the right direction and being photographed on the road, probably by the RNLI press officer from the station. The RNLI established Poole station in 1865 and it was celebrating over 150 years rescuing people at sea. The

Poole lifeboat station.

crew have been presented with 22 awards for gallantry. As Brenda and Brian were once again ahead of me I was anticipating a warm reception which is exactly what I received. After the initial cheers I had a nice warm cuppa and photographs were taken of the crew and me, filmed by Meridian Television. With Jim we left the station to walk the short distance to RNLI Headquarters with the crew surrounding us. This was a humbling but very satisfying moment.

On our arrival at the RNLI Headquarters and Training College the crowd was swollen by friends and relatives who had travelled down specially to be there at the end of what I can only describe as one of the most exciting and interesting things that I've ever done. There to meet us was Peter from the RNLI, my sister Ann and her husband Ray, their two neighbours Carol and Win, my son Tony, his fiancée Laura with her mother Jane. Tony and Laura presented Brenda and I with a glass of champagne and a glass trophy and Brian a smaller one. The presentation was filmed by Meridian while I was being interviewed. What a moment for me and my crew! To our surprise Brenda's parents arrived but they were a little late to witness the presentation but were in time for our tour around the College and a talk by volunteers telling us about the training and equipment they have on site. With them was my friend Frank and Brenda's brother David who had driven them down to meet us. After the tour we were invited to the restaurant where tea and sandwiches were laid on. This gave us the opportunity to catch up on each other's news. Tony, Laura and Jane with the dogs left for home around 5:30 pm and an hour later Brenda's brother and parents and Frank also left for home. Ann, Ray, Carol, Win, Brenda and myself remained to go into Poole for a walk around and eventually find somewhere for a meal. At around 8:30 pm Brenda, Brian and I returned to the caravan and the others left for home.

This whole project from its inception in my head to the very last day, I can only describe as one of the most exciting and interesting things that I have ever done. From the moment I started talking to people about my idea and seeing the wonderful reactions which they had to it, their enthusiasm adding to mine just kept on building up my excitement for the project. Then there had been the kindness of all the people who helped me with the planning and fundraising from local businesses and supporters from Edenbridge and the surrounding area – it had all given me the hope that I could put this project together and succeed in my aim.

Thank you everyone for your wonderful support and courage which gave me the chance to complete the project successfully and thanks too for the help and support of my wife Brenda and, of course, my friend Brian – without them it would never have happened. In the end both Brenda and I did not want the project to end because we had enjoyed the experience of meeting many members of the RNLI and the general public so much – not forgetting the beautiful coastline that Great Britain has to offer!

## August 14 – 17, Home/Epilogue

The end of a spectacular journey and a wonderful experience. On the morning of August 14th Brian left the site to travel home. He took the scooter with him to put in my garage on his way. Brenda and I were going to spend a few more days relaxing and visiting friends before returning ourselves. After helping Brian load his car and saying our goodbyes he left us. Not long after Brian had gone we were on our way to visit Mudeford. We stopped at the pub for a roast dinner before going back to the car park overlooking the Isle of Wight close to the RNLI lifeboat station. This was to soak up the atmosphere overlooking this busy shipping lane now that we were able to give ourselves time to take in the view.

On the morning of August 15th Brenda and I spent time reflecting on the journey that the three of us had managed to complete, the many challenges we that we had overcome, and the most satisfying thing of all – completing the project and raising £5,000 for the RNLI (although we missed the £10,000 target I was aiming for)! After breakfast it was now up to me to deal with all the utilities around the caravan; filling the water container, emptying the waste water and checking on the toilet, before we could leave the caravan, and visit our friends.

We drove to the RNLI College at Poole where we had our lunch and looked around the museum and shop. We then went and found our friends' house which was not far away and soon all four of us were on our way to visit Sandbanks millionaires' row. We parked there for a while and had a walk on the beach before returning to the car and driving down to their favourite fish-and-chip shop. We then drove back towards Poole stopping at a viewpoint where we sat with our fish and chips enjoying the view. We returned to their house where we spent the evening before returning to the caravan, ending an enjoyable day catching up with old friends.

August 16th was our last full day before we returned home. We visited the New Forest for the last time and returned to Calshot again, enjoying the view overlooking the Solent with the Isle of Wight in the distance. On the way back we stopped at a small lake for an ice cream. We then moved on and parked in a lay-by hoping to get close to some very small ponies. We were still reflecting on our epic journey and, in one respect, wanting it to continue but, in another, we were looking forward to seeing family and friends back home.

August 17th was a day of sadness now that it was all over but it was also a day of joy to be returning home. After the packing was done and the caravan firmly connected to the car we began our hundred-mile plus journey back. On our arrival we opened the front door to be greeted by balloons and a banner welcoming us back, put there by our wonderful family. Our next task was to empty the caravan of our possessions and tow it to a safe site before it was returned to Chichester Caravans. In the evening we invited family and friends to meet us at our local pub, the Old Eden in Edenbridge where we spent an enjoyable evening reminiscing with the family about what had taken place over the last 19 weeks we had spent on the road raising money for the RNLI.

Presenting a cheque at Hastings lifeboat station.

Later on, in 2012, when we were sure that all the money was in, we would be able to present a check to the RNLI of £5000 at Hastings lifeboat station.

Finally it leaves me to say how proud I am to have raised money for an organization that has volunteers saving lives. If you have bought this book it will mean more funds will go to this great organization as well as to the British Polio Fellowship. I will donate all the proceeds from the book to these worthy organisations.

# Acknowledgements

A very special thank-you to my wife Brenda, and my friend Brian for their help and support throughout this fantastic journey.

Huge thanks to Jim for the time and support he gave me organising this adventure. He was my right-hand man. Thanks to Lynda and Simon for their support and to Lynda especially for her hands-on help during our time in Scotland. Thanks also to Kev Reynolds for his help and advice in putting this book together and to Margaret Richards for her help in preparing the first draft. Thanks to my old school pals; Ian, Lesley, Toni and Marilyn. Thanks to my son Tony for his publicity efforts, particularly during our journey. Thanks to family, friends, and to neighbours, people that live in my home town of Edenbridge and surrounding areas, for all the donations and support they gave throughout the three years it took to put the project together.

A special thanks to Chichester Caravans for loaning the caravan and accessories, and to John, his wife and family, for looking after me so well during the time I spent with them at their house and at the NEC during the build-up for our trip. I will never forget their kindness; also that of all the people I met at the NEC during my two stays with John and his rep and all who were kind enough to donate in their different ways.

I must also show my appreciation to the company that supplied the scooter, Days Healthcare from South Wales, and to our website sponsors Greenmeanie, plus the company that provided the towbar, Westfalia UK Ltd., and to Jim, their Director. Thanks too to Whitmores of Edenbridge for fitting the towbar, and organising the wiring needed to complete this operation. I would also like to thank my friend Frank and his brother Chris who at their mother's funeral asked everyone to donate to our project Scoot4Life. I would also like to thank Crawley College and their students for their donation. Brenda and I were invited there to receive the cheque in person from the students which was a very humbling experience. I must also thank the Chailey Heritage Old Scholars Association for their kind donation and the support they gave us during the build-up to the project.

During this whole experience it is only through these people helping me in different ways and with my own determination that we were able to achieve success for this wonderful project. It was a fantastic experience for us and at the same time raised money for the RNLI.

This just leaves me to say, without all these people, the dream I had would have never have been realised. So if you have a dream, keep it alive, pursue it until you reach your goal, and never, never, give up.

Printed in Great Britain
by Amazon